Forgive me darkness, for living in light,

forgive me those, for I have been nothing more,

than a shadow in your lives.

"Lasciate ogne speranza, voi ch'intrate"

"Abandon all hope, ye who enter here"

To Hell I Go

by

Aaron Dalzell

It only gets worse...

The Depths Below:

Inferno Overture

†

Step forward, fire before my eyes,

let's keep going, the flames arise,

keep one step ahead, no turning back now.

Keep a foothold, the caverns lead me deeper,

and there's no coming back,

as is above, so it shall be below,

take another step and...

To hell I go!

Open the Dour

†

Try to open the door,

its rusted shut by blame and steam,

fires burn down beneath,

fury, rage, malice, discontent,

rivets melted, metal corroded,

this door will not open,

pry if you must, you have not strength enough,

to peer within, to release the pressure,

if only there were a key, a way,

to pry this immovable door away!

A closed in space,

four walls without a face,

no smiles, no tears, dreams black with fear,

a stern image peering into a mirror,

reflections chip and crack, there is no luck,

a humorless wreck,

post-partum zombie,

risen up after the anxiety attack,

without soul, without faith,

I was born here, this is my place,

no coming back...no escape!

My Darkness, My Love

†

Forgive me darkness...for living in light,

for there is no blindness,

when your shadows are visible to me,

at night I'm restless, at night I linger,

cool me with your cold, black love,

for the soothing touch fills me with chills,

the presence of somber demons fills me with laughter,

these voids where I needed the strength,

are filled by the fountains of doom, my haunter,

and my blood will drip with darkness,

when I cut, you will see, there is nothing more to hide,

because in my eyes, there is light no longer...

In Shadows, She Dwells

†

I wish I could love her,

but in shadows she dwells,

surrounded by cold air,

and that storm cloud looms,

inner demons, the alcohol consumes,

there is no light, where darkness is kept,

I only wish she could walk from those shadows,

and I could see her beauty in the daylight.

Phantasy
(Love Never Dies Part III)
†

I see her here, or is she just a fantasy,

is that her standing in the hall,

or is she just a phantom of my memories?

Her voice, it beckons,

but my blood runs cold,

this is not the love I remember,

I feel a chill upon my flesh by her tone.

"Come back to me,

my love, for I am here,

time has passed since we embraced,

to long has it been, too long I have waited..."

I stand silent, naked and alone,

within these halls, entrails of fiberglass,

centuries of separation by emotions made of stone,

who is this, she who speaks,

a banshee of her fallen throne?

Once I dreamed,

I had a vision in my mind,

of love with the woman of night,

and upon her black wings we took flight.

But now I am awake,

and the sensations feel so real,

that this vision of what love was,

has found me, but now...

I feel threatened, now I don't know what to do.

"Come back to me,

I am yours, the salvation you used to seek.

I am the love you dreamed of,

remember all the pleasure you offered me?"

I don't want to go,

for my emotions cannot follow,

what was once a dream, has faded,

and now my thoughts of her,

they feel so hollow.

"Come back to me,

I gave you pleasure, I gave you infinity,

you will return to me,

you are mine, we are one for eternity!"

My blood runs cold,

by this argument she keeps,

I belong to no one,

my body is mine, for dreams,

are only dreams.

She takes a step closer,

as the shadows in these halls surround me,

I feel her arms wrap around me,

and the hot breath upon my neck.

"I have returned,

I've come to claim what is mine,

I wanted to share the world with you,

but now...I sense something different,

I don't understand the thoughts in your mind..."

I push her away,

the taste of blood unsettles me,

the thoughts of ruling in darkness,

a day without a sun to rise,

these dreams, are nightmares in reality.

"So...that is how it is to be,

no longer do we share the passion, the love,

to drink the blood of infinity,

life is what you truly desire,

for I, your queen,

am just a phase, a faded memory,

then I release you, and forget what was to be,

there is no ecstasy to be gained,

you are not the one I thought you'd be."

"It seems that love has died this day,

but there are others, who call to me,

I will take my leave,

please, no longer think of me,

no longer dream of me,

no more calls, no more fantasies,

I leave you here,

now let fate take you on its course,

and find true meaning behind your remorse."

"Your eyes are awake,

your wanderlust has seen the way to a new horizon,

I hope you find the love you seek,

as for what you dream,

find the meaning for your love's remorse,

leave me behind, and forget the memories...."

"...leave behind, the passion you once held for me."

And Though I Walk

†

And though I walk,

and the shadows are with me,

they move unseen,

but I see them, they surround me,

nightmares of hostility,

demons and daemonic beings, so obscene,

too horrific for their secrets to be revealed,

they've called my name long ago,

and I've obliged, their spokesman,

to represent all evil in the killing fields,

for within these valleys of the mind,

walk with me, and to you,

these familiar evils...will call you too!

Where's the Light

†

Wishing, for another day

looking up…at the sky,

can't see tomorrow, can't see across…

Time

Can't see my guiding light,

where's the light,

where's the light,

While I'm wishing for the future to carry me,

when I should be sleeping,

instead I twist and turn at night.

Wondering, about tomorrow,

wondering, if I try,

can't make it through the day,

can't see without my…

Light

Where's my guide,

where's Virgil?

where's the light,

where's the light,

While I'm hoping others will wait for me,

when I should be focused,

I should have peace of mind!

Wondering, what I've forgotten,

are they, lost to time,

can't remember yesterday,

can't remember what's on my...

Mind

Just need a moment,

I'm blinded by the night,

where's the light,

where's the light,

While I look at photos and write in the diary,

when I should have been there,

I wish I spent more time.

When I look back on my past,

when I look back on my life,

there's nothing there but a young boy,

shrouded by the shadows of night.

The Gothic City

†

I feel the night,

is always after me,

wails from the afterlife,

calling me away, screaming for me,

beyond the forest of silence,

and the shadows filled with valleys,

upon the horizon, past the mist,

over haunted plateau-filled nightmares,

the gothic city beckons me,

can anyone hear them?

or is it just me,

can anyone see the eyes watching,

from the alleys of the gothic city?

I walk the streets,

is there anyone with me?

a pebble echoes down the road,

ahead of me,

I feel I'm not alone,

there is always something with me,

haunting me,

driving me by night,

through the streets,

of the gothic city.

Shadowhold

†

Do you know them?

Have you seen them?

Have you felt those hands?

They live in the shadows,

they follow us all our lives,

they feast on emotional anxiety,

they hunt us down for our happiness.

Just when I'm feeling good,

enjoying the evening, enjoying the day,

that's when they come, to take me away.

And yet again I see those hands,

creeping from the black, crawling across the land,

coming for me, trying to drag me back.

Twisted claws reach out from the shadows,

taking light from my serenity,

reaching out to take me back,

to spend more time in the lair of the black.

And yet again, I see those hands,

creeping black, from the shadows emerge the hands,

old grudges, new enemies, and bad memories,

they return to torment me.

A Darker Reflection

†

In the centuries when we began,

I remember,

the days of yesteryear,

when we built with our hands,

when we thought with our minds,

when we bled, for what we believed.

"A time when actions,

spoke louder than words."

A time when we brought,

all these elements, the five senses together,

a symphony of builders and architecture,

and created something colossal,

something fresh and new,

every little piece, was part of something larger.

A vast and mighty stronghold,

the greatest of all civilizations,

wealth was plenty, we passed it all around,

weary souls came from out-of-bounds,

we welcomed them back into the game,

the meek and the down-trodden,

so they could see for themselves,

these citadels, they could help themselves,

what was ours we shared,

a mentor, a role-model,

to our youth,

for what we were about.

"And as to me, I do to you!
As to all, so to all of you!"

Now only fragments,

of what we once stood for,

before we buried our castles,

and all our people,

in the ground.

"I am in evolution—"

"Evolution is a theory...not fact!"

"The mind over mammals!"

Flames and false prophets,

burned all we've known,

influence altered pictures,

words altered speech,

memories we once kept hold,

are now memories we desperately seek.

War changed our ways,

fate rises like a phoenix from the ash,

while bodies stay buried in the rubble,

from battles that left ancient ruins,

places we once called our own.

"Farewell to everyone,

farewell to home—"

In the cracked mirror,

the glass we broke,

with the pound of our fist,

we face the darker side of the reflection,

the reality we try to hide.

The reflection reveals,

our behavior, our psychology,

our sociology, our theology,

our lies and our apologies,

the mirror shows us what we are.

What are we? We're humankind.

Is it coming back to you?

The Bitter Face

†

See him?

I do...the bitter face,

of a poor man, a blighted sapien,

getting by on fumes, barely nothing left,

alters destiny on a massive level,

stares through shards of a broken mirror,

who is he?

Who knows...who cares,

just another bitter face in the crowd,

just another sad misfit passing by,

looking around at what there is,

glaring through enraged eyes,

and that face with a dreaded cringe,

now he's looking inside himself,

bitter about what he should have been,

what he could have been,

a friend to others he should have been,

selfish and angry at the mess he's in,

self-centered, crying on no one's shoulder,

there's no one there,

now he's looking down the cross,

now he's looking past the hope,

now he's facing the fires below,

looking down at what they call hell,

but it's punishment, it's his doing,

and the anger's rising,

a penance to atone for,

and the longer he looks, the more he stares,

the noose gets tighter, the fires get higher,

the rope slides lower,

how much lower can he go?

I guess he'll burn,

and the pieces will melt away,

once he's crumbled,

once there's nothing left,

no more bridges left to burn,

what more is there for him to loose,

he's lost it all,

can there be any forgiveness?

I don't think so,

there's none left around him,

to entertain, to try and make them smile,

one growl, one roar,

and the mean old snarl has scared them all away,

chasing shadows, of those he lost,

of the people that were once there,

now there's no one,

and so this bitter man,

can glare and glare and glare,

all he wants, he can do it forever,

if he chooses,

because this bitter man,

is a lonely man,

because now,

no one cares...

Self —

†

A small deadly space,

closed in by barbwire,

locks welded shut upon the gate,

I never get out, no escape, never let anyone in,

rabid dogs bark at the intruders,

once familiar faces, now strangers,

property forbidden, grass crumbled and dead,

never mowed and never tended,

lost among the gloom and doom,

alone and forsaken, no more care taken,

soil is rotten, lights burned out,

"Go away! I'm never leaving!"

I linger inside, worthless and wheezing,

cigarette's glow, keeps burning, covers the scarring,

muscles old, lungs are failing, body's aching,

"Go away! There's no more dreaming!"

Bound within walls with electrical rage pulsating,

kept trapped, kept a self-abomination,

there's no more space in here for hope or moving,

for any satisfaction,

don't want to come outside, detest the sun,

too distracted by thoughts of self-mutilation,

no more concern for the living,

a prisoner of anger, held in by its domination,

"Go away! And leave this wicked creation!"

There's no room in here for your pity,

for support, for friendship, for serenity...

Incorporeal Vices

†

What we can't see,

can hurt us more,

than any knife or sword,

the incorporeal vices seep deeper,

cutting wounds deeper and deeper and deeper,

scorn and avarice,

lies and deceit,

sadness and sorrow,

pain and mourning,

rage and anger,

jealousy and envy

these are the vices that taint,

existing deep down within,

these are our vices used to annihilate,

disintegrate, exterminate, obliterate,

where true damage is done,

I'd rather take a punch in the face,

because after a while,

that type of pain heals,

while incorporeal vices linger,

these are the vices that taint.

The Scar that Never Goes Away

†

The scar that never goes away,

is the memory that unfolds before us,

for it is this animosity we remember,

the true pain that never goes away.

But are all these memories,

truly bad or is it what we've made them?

For do we create the pain,

or is it born into us,

is it...innate?

Nothing Left but the Bones

†

Payments due, sacrifices to make,

traverse the vast and endless concrete,

roads broken and paved,

what will be left, when I reach my destination.

And I head on through the toll,

as another part of me is sold,

start with the flesh, peel it back,

watch the vices work their way,

down to the bone.

What will be left?

At the end of the road,

wear and ruin by the time I reach,

the final destination.

And I head on through the toll,

give another piece, another part sold,

taken the flesh, now finish what's begun,

soon there will be nothing left,

but the bones.

One by One

†

One by one,

I pick it all apart,

no chance to apologize,

no chance to redeem,

like a spider's legs,

I pull them off,

and leave it there to crawl,

as I walk away and never look back,

never apologize, never lend a hand,

I see a flaw in the system,

I see a defect in the grand plan,

I pick apart the details and leave the desiccation behind,

leave it there to struggle alone,

no room in my life,

for faults that could undermine my own...

Falling Man

†

This man dares to walk out to the edge.

One who never lived once, should have taken that step,

now he'll take the risk, but repeat it all over again,

adrenaline and anxiety,

shoots through the veins of a falling man,

falling again and again and again,

failing again and again and again,

falling all over again and again and again.

Continue on and for what?

To keep falling again and again and again?!

The Only Way...is Down
†

Each step I take, the higher I go,

the more the rungs shake, the more the ground,

beneath this ladder quakes,

there was never a structure,

to hold firmly in place, but I can't turn back,

the further up I go, I dare not look down,

no time for fear, for life is worse than a nightmare,

and dreams more disappointing than hope,

at last I reach, that pinnacle where I've longed to be,

but when I look down, look around,

I'm disappointed, I'm dizzy, I'm angry,

there is nothing else around, nothing left,

all drive has left a hollowed me, tired and empty,

there's nothing up here,

I thought there'd be opportunity,

but there's nowhere to go, and nothing to see,

no one to congratulate me, no longer encouraging,

all the voices, of the people past and present,

have left me at the beginning,

abandoned me half way through this climb,

or just never took the chance,

to be a part of my timeline,

this struggle upwards, means nothing to me this time,

achievements, success...means,

nothing, worthless at best,

maybe I've gone too far,

to a place that's left them all behind,

a place where this boy turns old, and this bled old man,

his only reward, his legacy,

is a heart corroded into weathered stone,

no more can I feel the cold,

no more can I feel the harsh wind,

nothing left to loose, cause in life I never win.

I walk out slowly towards the edge,

nothing to stop me,

it's either jump or linger as the living dead,

looking down these dizzying heights,

to the rocks below,

and my legs tremble, and the ladder breaks,

and it's down I go, spiraling out of control,

to join the other failures that left this world,

they checked out when they knew it was time to go.

I guess I feel I've gone on too long,

and this lifetime is stale and expired,

I have nothing more to offer, just let this old man retire,

I'm worn out...I'm tired,

no want for compassion,

only this innate tendency to be removed,

this ladder's been rusted, this time it's fallen,

and I'm not gonna fix it,

nor is there money to replace it,

I have no energy to get back up,

life's passed me by, I'm through.

Felon of Himself

†

"Pity the lunatic fringe,

poring over the lexicon to find,

a euphemism for suicide..."

The only light,

that shines in his life,

is the gleam upon metal,

glistening off the surface,

of the sharp edge, under the bathroom light,

the fine line between the decision,

of life, of death,

deceased or to persist?

The burn, and the pain of rejection bleeds away,

at the surface, it's all just surface pain,

mocking, laughing, misunderstanding,

never listening...never forgiving,

it's ok now, just one cut and all that pain will soon fade,

just a tap upon life's most precious vein,

smooth kiss of metal, watch the red drip consistently,

it's all just surface pain, everyone and himself to blame,

a little scratch turns to a wider incision,

a greater decision,

of life, of death,

deceased or to persist?

It's all just surface pain, perhaps mirror vain,

because what's underneath is numb,

no longer feeling, without a care for anything,

this little instrument, holds a man's fate,

a little slice and he will sleep, for the first time in life,

a little drop of blood,

and he'll pass quietly from all the strife,

these actions taken, asks the greater question,

of life, of death,

shall he proceed...to no longer be?

If you ask that man, what has life meant to him?

"Simply put...nothing...it means nothing...

a coward is...a coward I shall always be..."

Behind Closed Shades

†

Who is this face, that sits behind closed shades,

his face grotesque, marred and afraid,

shunned by the lowly, outcast to the world,

keep those sinister eyes hidden,

behind closed shades, to avoid the guilt bothering you,

behind closed shades,

do you eat the insects,

eye them up as your victims crawl?

Behind closed shades,

do you bind & torture,

maim & kill,

taking pleasure in the innocent blood you spill?

Behind closed shades,

hide your darkness from the world!

Behind closed shades,

what's your heart's deepest desire?

What's your thrill?

Behind closed shades,

do you empower, do you rule?

Behind the curtains and the lashes,

what kind of sadism pacifies you?

Behind black curtains,

keeping out the daylight,

what kind of animal,

what kind of savagery burns in those eyes?

Is it torture?

Is it gratification?

Eye up your target,

eat them away in your mind,

you creep upon them...gruesomely I may add,

but what would that face of theirs show,

if they saw you...what would they think of you?

A sadist, a creeper if you will.

Behind closed shades,

what sorts of gruesome acts are on his or her mind?

Behind closed shades,

what types of sick fucks,

are hidden away from everyday humankind?!

Man O' Vore

†

Voracious PIG!

Gorge if you will,

you glutton,

you devourer,

an appetite insatiable,

a sex drive that is unshakable!

You beat, you maim,

you steal then procreate!

To you, life is nothing more,

than a drinking game!

Your nothing more than a sow in the pen,

poultry to be slaughtered, meat to be butchered,

by the sickle of time, this butcher knife of mine,

gorge upon the innocent some more, and soon,

you'll be ready for the chopping block,

then by the jaws of the mangler, you'll be consumed!

Whorifice

†

In this day-n-age, what do you expect,

trying to listen, but the ears become deaf,

the nostrils smell the smoke, and the sacrifice is burning,

the mouth is open, but the words are not poetic,

as the shit is putrid, from the anus,

our words are shit, and we take a whiff,

from every conversation—

Soon we'll all be pissed away,

fecal cities fallen to decay,

lives so shitty while the surface is so pretty,

nothing can be done,

take the raping every day.

Smell so bad from the eruption,

human kind is no longer breathing.

It's time to close up shop,

and stop the trading that's perpetuating.

We don't want it anyway, we don't care anyway...

Theme Park
(The Carnalval o' Charades)
†

Idiots play charades,

when walking to the next ride, another line,

the next detention block for fun in sight,

led to the altar,

led along in the ungodly lines,

blistered in the heat, bask in the herd and their stench,

from body odor, boiled flesh from the water rides,

watch the cripples, watch the rejects,

come to have a high,

they can never get in life,

bring the families, bring the kids,

to an altered paradise,

of spinning wheels and twisted metal pipes,

an altered paradise, an illusion that doesn't exist,

a paradise to get your six-second injection,

cheap thrills and cheap prizes,

a false sense of worth,

a false prophecy, that you were a winner in this game,

come on up and claim your worthless prize,

a false sense of satisfaction,

an impedance of happiness that can no longer rise,

come on up and take your prize,

you waited in the line, you rode up and down,

the metal serpent's spine,

you had your fix, went along for the ride,

now the day is done, your climax...was it all worth it?

What's next, when you leave the hooker's gates,

drive to the next place, the next circus,

drag along your ego, drag along your family,

an orgy to the idiots, a ménage a trois,

to please them all, to please yourself,

caught up in the fun land to leave behind,

the real-world guilt,

but does the quickie,

do the cheap thrills,

the penny arcades and the dirty restrooms,

the asses in the seats,

the bumper car rides,

does that look of pleasure on their face,

that cheap thrill,

in the long run,

does it truly satisfy?

Out of Order

†

Pack your bags, head for the hills,

someone shook hands and we made the deal,

more, more, more, and all for free,

a little pig went to the market, that pig is liberty.

Out of Order,

you better get your shit together,

Out of Order,

because we're on the frontier of a new disorder!

Grab it off the shelves, can't get enough,

we don't even want it, but we love this stuff,

so many choices and no money to pay,

but don't you worry, it'll be half-off the next day.

Out of Order,

can't accept sloppy when we drive the speed,

Out of Order,

we make a mess with all the sweat we bleed!

If they don't want it, we'll reinstate it,

call it something different,

won't be long, before those idiots take it!

Out of Order,

a bunch of mice without the traps,

Out of Order,

chasing our tails, we're doing laps!

This world is...mechanized,

institutionalized, digitally certified...

This world is...a storm,

an explosion, a plague, a massive wave...

This world is...upside-down, inside-out, ass-backwards...

Out of Order,

hanging by the neck of all our discord,

Out of Order,

we bite the hand and pant like dogs for our rewards!

Fingernails

†

Grandmother's visage,

rocks upon her fallen throne,

where ghosts haunt in steps,

follow children to their rooms,

creep into their dreams at night,

hide in closets and under beds,

grandmother's demons follow,

inherited into impressionable minds.

"Creak...Creak...Creak..."

Echoes these footsteps down the hall,

echoes shadows of the night,

creep across the floor,

long fingers reach out from the dark,

screams paralyzed in sleep,

no warning, reaching for us,

to grasp a hold before we wake...

Siren's Cull

†

Upon desolate shores, beyond reefs under waves,

where all ships wash up, for the women of myth,

to feast, and upon the tide, the remains wash away.

Hear their call in the dark, in nightmares,

a desperate, insane man's fragile, confused mind,

they call me by name, and I must obey.

I leave no trace of myself behind,

no proof that I once existed, as I take the next ship,

upon the next tide I sail...to that land beyond.

Where the dreaded sirens...sing and wail!

There's A Sayin'

†

Innocent Blood

-

There's a sayin' in these parts,

a rural legend,

livin' within these here woods,

that the old crow in the back country,

likes to eat little boys and girls.

Yep...she'll put a spell on yah,

if she can,

look into them their eyes,

and yer fates now in her hands!

Folks say she likes fresh meat,

so we feed her raw steaks,

keep slabs of bloodied beef,

fresh, on the borders of the back country,

it keeps her away,

because when she's hungry,

she'll a come a creepin' along,

she'll come out of the woods,

and watch from the bushes,

as the children go outside and play,

…at least, they used to go outside,

now we keep them indoors,

while those steaks of our livestock,

keep that 'ol witch away for now.

But she's a cunning one,

Oh! She's a brazen,

now she stalks our sheep and chickens,

comes a creepin' out of the woods,

around somewhere between midnight,

and just before mornin',

old Pap Savage saw her the other night,

chewin' on the skin of his chickens,

and chokin' up the feathers,

he shot at her twice, both barrels of his shotgun,

he shot twice,

she must move pretty quick,

because he missed,

not even a drop of blood,

except for the blood of the chickens.

It won't be long before she comes,

creepin' round my land,

but I'll be a ready,

you just wait and see,

she comes creepin' round my farm,

me, my wife and our little daughter,

she'll get more than she bargained for,

I got my traps set, got my buck-shot ready,

ready to fill her full of lead!

And I'll stay up all night,

I won't sleep,

until that no good witch is dead!

The mistress of the ravens,

the queen of the ebony crown,

perched upon her dominion,

feathers outstretched about to take flight,

the gurgle echoes down her throat,

as she swallows that final bite of flesh,

the final drink of blood, and the bones are tossed away,

piled upon the decrepit brick beneath her feet,

along with all the remains...of the little ones,

and their toys and ripped-away clothes,

and then...the doors to the towers burst open,

she hears the mobs and villagers down below,

their coming...to stake the witch,

and burn this bitch away,

the killer of innocence...the eater of children flies away!

The rustic doors burst open, and they look,

take in the horror that's all around,

all that's left of the ones they loved,

taken away by this beast that stalks from above,

and I heard, by those that were there,

they claimed, all that was left, was their possessions,

as far as the children...nothing left remained...

Eater of Children

She ate them all,

she filled her belly,

she's escaped, she's loose,

she's up there somewhere,

running...flying...escaping...avoiding!

Will we ever see her again?

She's out there somewhere...hunting,

terrorizing in other parts out there.

She's gone, but her shadow still lingers,

even after we burned down the tower.

We remain silent in these parts,

keep our lips shut to outsiders...to strangers,

we don't talk about her anymore,

that witch...that abomination,

that there creature that ate our children!

Rise of the Leviathan
†

Arise,

from beneath the seas,

the empty haul, where the echoes scream!

Arise,

from under blood-red tides,

after the sea-monsters had their feast!

Arise,

once a symbol of tyrants and animosity,

from a restless sleep, and nightmares filled with pain!

Arise,

titan of destruction, machine of annihilation,

a testament of persecution and extinction!

Arise,

Leviathan, for the time has once again come,

to spread your anarchy and disdain!

Once thought drowned in a raging sea,

the Leviathan once again rises,

to continue its campaign of death and misery!

Dragonist

†

Deceptive serpents raise their necks,

above the bones and fallen monoliths,

beyond the realms of life and death,

their many faces and fiery breath,

observe all who follow down the wrong path.

Flesh eaters, mind readers,

they know every move we make,

smell every breath we take,

taste every bead of sweat from our mistakes.

Reptilian eyes watch as a lone wanderer,

enters into their mists, walks untrodden paths,

meet head-on, the snakes wreathed in flames,

"come closer to us foolish one! just a little closer,

accept your folly, confront your fate!"

These dreaded prophets of forgotten age,

whisper fear that reaches out beyond their gates,

for this is the last stand, the final stage,

a thousand heads circulate, to focus in one direction,

which makes the all-wise, blinded to their fall,

cast back in the lake's reflection.

Many eyes see one vision, and lose sight,

of what's been forgotten, while a solitary mind,

of many thoughts ponder on, always recollects,

the hurt in the past that's happened.

He, this wanderer, chose this path,

he came this way for a reason,

to fix those broken bones,

which lay dead and unforgiven,

covered over by the mists,

claws latch upon his shoulders, slumped by the weight,

of bloody jaws, of slashing nails,

he came this way last time,

he chose to do so, and he'll walk,

this road again and again,

this is the wanderer's fate.

Only...this time he is prepared, he has learned,

from each left turn taken, it was right!

Again he has mistaken,

but he holds his strength, he keeps an iron will,

and once he finds the way, and takes a stance to fight,

these fowl creatures, he will conquer, he swore to kill,

and this time...the time is nigh...it feels right!

And with each path taken, lessons have been learned,

discoveries are made, like steel forged into the blade,

chips and dents peel the armor back, break the iron will,

but wrongs will be forgiven...he must! he shall!

With each wrong turn, he'll face another beast,

another monster will have risen,

and when he comes face to face with,

those jaws that chew and break,

another dragon's head...again and again...he will take!

The Hymn

And behold,

a giant arises from the ranks ahead,

to overshadow a future that's uncertain,

and until one stands ground and fights back,

to bring the giant down, overthrow the behemoth,

the shadow of doubt, will conquer the land.

An iron fist clenches,

only a stronger hand can break,

years of past emotions,

that have left a kingdom on the brink.

And behold,

the giant stands among many,

claiming this domain his own,

and all within for the taking,

and until the youth matures, and stands and realizes,

the mistakes he's making, chances he's not taking,

to face against such a demoralizing foe,

can you feel the earth shaking?

In his mind, war-drums beating?!

The firm grip that clenches,

begins to tremble, and loses its strength,

as years of emotions have had enough,

and announce its time to break away!

And so behold,

as from behind these lines, of scared and beaten faces,

a young man once nameless and hidden,

makes his stand,

against a foe more terrifying,

than a thousand nightmares,

more deadly than any blade, more toxic than poison,

a little boy stands the test of time, to face this giant,

a foe ageless as time,

a foe who hurts...outside and inside,

a loser becomes a winner, a coward becomes a hero,

as years of oppression is beaten...in a single blow!

The clenched-fist loosens,

the grasp of rage drops its spear,

that has been driven into the heart,

every day...every year!

And behold,

this boy...is now a man, a warrior, a king,

no more running, he has fought for his promised land,

to free himself and others,

from this cold and bitter hand,

a tale for the books, and legends to be told,

the retelling of a classic tale, a confessor's mold,

of inspired revolution, over a grip that had its hold,

over a child that was hurt, is now letting go,

to anger that had taken him...and cries out to all,

"VEXATION, ANIMOSITY, INDIGNATION!

LET THIS VICTIM GO!"

Lead him to the places,

where there are better crops to sow...

Death of a Monster

Does the blood still run through it,

Are fingers slick upon the blade?

Let go the weapon...it's over,

fallen is the rampage,

as life fades away.

Slain for crimes of animosity,

there is no glory, there is no reward to reap,

for the scars and slashes of battle stain the walls,

and around, the beaten are piled high,

hopeless and left to die.

And once its body ceases to breath,

once and for all... just maybe,

the beast...at last, has fallen!

Her Wounds

†

Her wounds,

came from the same source as her power,

she bleeds to heal others,

she dies to save others,

her sacrifices are for the greater good,

if only others understood,

if only they could...

Bled Rose

(Lady of the Night 2)

†

Innocent for the taking,

upon sheets drenched,

soon to be oceans, folds form mountains,

walls keep the shame from leaving,

keeps the guilt within after the harvesting.

Prisoners taken, victims forsaken,

to gardens of thorns,

bound for the taking after the bidding,

bodies left slaughtered,

a cruel wake-up call after the slaying.

Roses are red, violence black and blue,

whispers are sweet, lies are cruel,

beg to the end, the final exhalation,

left to mourn, drenched sheets scorched and torn,

love once felt good, until deceit ripped between,

and the bled rose has lost its petals,

left for dead, exposed, and wilted,

the rose once red, the rose is now bled,

violence is black and blue, deceit hides love from view,

all that's left, a trail of dirt...a long road of mirth,

to follow, to swallow,

a tattoo of stains to consume...

and leave the flesh hollow.

Victims and all the blaming,

trials and fines, slaps on the wrist,

just another name scratched off a list,

head held over a pit of maiming,

hanging high, gasping for air,

left helpless, with body swinging,

no more care, no more sounds to be heard,

covered over by all the screaming,

and come the morning, there will be no more weeping.

A rose once red...now pale and white as snow,

bled of life, though once a happy gal,

the violence cruel, the feeling of love exhumed,

to keep from view, the shame she can never undo.

Blood Swan
(The Return of Red Barbie)
†

I hear her, the sirens cull,

another victim torn down,

piece by piece into the depths,

beneath crimson tides.

Any last words, a futile wale,

a call up to the godless skies,

and her pearly-white smile,

reflects within their dying eyes,

as she jests their prayers and cries...

"Please God! I don't want to die!"

And the blood swan drifts along,

with the cold winds she sails,

her luring call echoes still,

as she spreads her wings and flies,

this succubus, this butcher of the night.

Her laugh, a child's giggle,

as her victims struggle and wiggle,

red lipstick upon their cheek,

a sweet kiss by the dainty beast,

as into their conscious, the predator speaks...

"Hi...

You know the worst fear of humans,

attacks the flesh, but scars the brain,

the Emperor of the Black Crown is my lord,

and I the red queen, a scratch of my nails,

and the flesh, it crawls with the pleasure of the sting,

doesn't it, my rapture over you, holds you within,

my kingdom, my blood-red womb,

to cradle and protect you, keep you near,

poor wretched man, do not fear,

for I have returned, and I know,

I know what all mankind desires,

yes...yes I do,

so we can make this painless,

we, my love, we can make this erotic,

we can have fun, the time of my life,

we can make this song last forever,

think about it...the bloodiest swan song of all time!"

Last Supper
†

The guards take a stroll,

to take a gander down upon,

the avenues and causeways of death row,

gaze upon the faces of ghosts,

sunken and white as skeletons in the deep.

They come to the furthest cell,

where solitaire is in confinement,

they insert the key and turn the lock,

and with a crack, into her lair they walk,

and she beckons, she looks upon them,

with that familiar sweet, sweet smile.

"Hello there, come on in...the water's fine!"

She laughs and giggles,

an echo that brings a dreaded fear to the others,

she does it every night, along with howl at the moon,

they can't wait to see her go,

"Take this lunatic away! Let us ponder,

these last few moments in peace upon death row!"

The guards turn to each other,

that wide eyed look of confusion,

watching the chained woman splash her face,

with water as cold as ice, from a rusted faucet,

this water can never clean this monster's face,

can never wash all the blood from her victims' away.

"Tomorrow's a big day for you."

The guard says, and the woman's face lights up,

"It is?! Is it my birthday, is it Easter...is it Christmas!

Hanukah...Ramadan...No, don't tell me...

I want to guess...ah I know,

It's Candlemass! It's Blackmass! Oh how I wish,

I wish these wonderful holidays would last!

In celebration of blood and violence...

when all these men and women kill each other,

I wish I was not locked up and I could join them!"

She laughs.

"Oh, we could play such fun games,

see who can slaughter the most unbelievers...

the most deceivers...the most people! Ohhh jooooyyy!"

73

They grasp her by the shoulders,

and throw her back to the wall,

"It's neither you crazy bitch!

It's the day we strap you to the chopping block,

the day when we put you down,

and you won't kill anymore!"

She grasps her bleeding head, she looks at the blood,

and begins to sob and cry,

"You mean...I won't see this anymore?!"

She holds her hand up, covered in blood and hair.

"I...I won't see the pretty red anymore?"

And she sobs some more.

"Your through Barbie...your done!

No more killing for you...your being punished,

I think you should be tortured like your victims!"

And Barbie thinks back, smiling,

reminiscing on those good 'ol times,

the slaughter, the laughter,

all the blood, all the fun,

all the screaming...all the daydreaming.

"Tomorrow we're gonna put you down,

and we're gonna take great pride in it,

great satisfaction, in seeing you dead!

I think we should burn her alive,

what about you?"

The guard turns to the other,

"I think we should beat her now,

giver her more of that "pretty red" she wants,

make her lick it...make her eat it, make her choke on it!"

She gets excited, *"I like the pretty red...tastes like salt!"*

The guards grasp the steel batons,

they swat it against their palms, until their raw,

until their nice and red,

they surround Barbie, grinning, chuckling.

"Consider this your last supper...I hope you like it!"

And throughout the night,

they beat her, they maim her,

they take the flesh off her back, make it nice and red,

they slam and hit, *"WOOSH"* and *"SMACK,"*

as they drive the weapons down,

they bruise her, they clobber her,

they rip the clothes from her body,

they break the bones, they fracture the skull,

one takes out a large knife,

while the other holds her down.

She screams, she cries and wails,

the prisoners rattle their cages,

wanting it to stop, wanting this nightmare to go away,

they lay her hand flat against the harsh cement,

first, they chop the fingertips away,

then they get greedy,

they feel the bloodlust, they feel the drive,

they cut away finger after finger, then the palm,

the pool of red grows, under Barbie's bloody nub.

She screams and she howls, but no one's coming,

not till dawn, not till dawn.

"The RED...It burns...It burns...it hurts me!"

They laugh at her, mock her,

"Oh...does it hurt?! Well just you wait you bitch,

It's gonna get so much worse!"

Many hours passed, what else they did to her,

cannot be described,

but when she was found the next day...

the morning guard found her splayed, hung up,

her skin wide open and chest exposed,

she had traces of urine and stool within her cuts,

her bruises poisoned, her lesions infected,

the welts and slashes all across her back and face,

unrecognizable, horrific acts upon her,

deemed unthinkable!

Her perpetrators? They got away,

they got greedy, their bloodlust unsatisfied,

not finished with their own genocide!

As for Red Barbie...they drug the body away,

instead of the executioner's blade,

they stuck her in the mortician's oven,

and the smoke that arose in the sky on that day,

ran red...with the blood of slaughter,

the death and mayhem that,

consumed her, destroyed her,

surrounded her, excited her, drove her,

but no longer,

as the urban legend of Red Barbie,

is burned away,

but when one terror is eviscerated,

another one rises up to take its place.

Black Obsidian Fence

†

Rancor,

that's what this feeling is,

this is not the life,

these are not the golden years,

for a life of living in hell,

is spent behind bars, jailed within,

a house of smoke, a heavy air,

a thick atmosphere,

can you taste the anger,

can you lick the pain,

give the children melted ice cream,

watch their dreams as they drip away,

feed them on their leashes, clothing rots,

as these minds crumble like dirt,

as these dreams are crushed, held back,

chased away, like the dogs,

they behave, beatings they obey,

dare to chance a dance with the beast,

dare to cross the perimeter,

trespass upon the property, the brown grass crunches,

the black obsidian fence,

keeps them locked within,

stakes of iron keep lives that are worthless,

lives wishing they could be free,

lives within hoping,

a ray of the outside light that never comes,

wanting to taste the air from an open door,

dirty faces and subjugated minds,

wanting to see what's out there,

to be on the other side...

Grinding Teeth

†

Am I asleep again?

Is that the feeling of grinding teeth,

or is this the roar of a gritting beast?

Saliva sloshes around upon my teeth,

licking my lips after the feast,

blood runs thick...do you remember?

Blood runs thick down the throat of the beast!

Ain't It Funny

✝

The battles I've fought,

as hard as I've tried,

ain't it funny, I'm all burned out,

and stepped on like the cigarette on the ground,

can't get anywhere on time,

when crawling on hands and knees across the ground.

All accomplishments, all I've done,

ain't it funny, it's all been backwards and wrong!

Wasn't that amusing...funny?

Well, I'm not laughing now,

staring down into this grave,

six feet underground.

And these...these animals,

some call humans, they refer to themselves as,

this species called people,

I look at them, zooming and drooling all around,

pathetic aren't they, I look at them,

and I'm...I'm so confound!

As hard as I try,

honest work doesn't get by,

as these worthless reap the spoils,

and laziness, dishonesty, these are our chosen,

we hand them the keys to humankind.

Judgment decided by a lower idiocracy,

imbeciles to lead as their mistakes will make us bleed,

break bones, break backs, break necks,

as the shoulders pull trying to haul another stack.

Ain't it funny, those who try to push ahead,

get tossed further and further back.

Decision making is a morons game,

as the mentally declined lead the blind,

and the mute speak to the deaf,

nobody hears, nobody understands,

the miscommunication, nor the typos with the red line,

nobody bothers caring anymore,

except for me, myself, and I.

But I'll stand back,

and just watch these funny creatures,

keep on rushing by, just hustle on their way,

heads up their crevices, eyes on tiny screens,

not on what they're doing, where they're going,

their world only a gigabyte large,

and a flat-screen wide.

Ain't it funny, not when you see them,

flesh and blood becomes pixels and wires,

truth punished, and we celebrate liars.

We've become a different kind of machine,

it's not funny, when you see...when you know,

there's nothing left of us, there is no future

no money to be made in humanity.

Rawr

†

Hear the cry,

of my blood-curdling scream!

"Raaawwwrrr!"

Hear the roar of a man,

about to decimate to the extreme!

"Raaawwwrrr!"

I scream, you scream,

they all scream when they hear...

"Raaawwwrrr!"

My pounding, my stomping,

my thrashing, my killing!

"Raaawwwrrr!"

I carve my way through bodies,

I silence the weeping, butcher the fleeing!

"Raaawwwrrr!"

Scream bloody gore,

shriek as loud as you can,

"Raaawwwrrr!"

No one can hear you scream anymore,

no one survives my slaughter, when you hear...

"Raaawwwrrr!"

Times wasting,

you better start running!

The Black and Blood

†

Brutal retaliation,

retribution a blinding storm,

soldiers in formation,

pummel the faces into their skulls more and more!

Feel not forgiveness,

have no shame and no regret,

we belong to the black and blood,

soldiers of anarchy,

soldiers bred for mayhem and death!

Hateful annihilation,

anger a raging stampede,

walk the streets, slaughter all in our path,

psycho killers wielding axes and machineguns!

Have no remorse,

for we shall show none once you're dead,

we belong to the black and blood,

storm-troopers out for the hunt,

track down all who live and destroy them!

Bring down the retribution,

for none stand in our way,

once normal everyday civilians,

now trained in terroristic combat,

for a single goal...a single purpose...

We're the legions of the black and blood,

on a genocidal campaign to exterminate,

and we'll kill the weak,

then we'll make the world bleed!

Xtinction Blues

†

Oh, how sad,

we ain't gonna be here no more,

cry all you want, tears don't heal the scourge.

Oh, go on and cry,

finally, a hint of sincerity,

in an otherwise insincere human,

cry all you want, we're all gonna die!

Oh, feeling a little down are we?

After all the luxury and the wasting,

it can't last forever, are we that surprised?

Hoping for an afterlife?

Hoping for thy kingdom come way up high?

That's the biggest lie, because when I look up,

all I see is the nukes in the sky,

prepare for war, prepare...we're all gonna die!

And when no one is left,

no longer will the humans whine...

The Night the Inferno Came

†

I remember that night,

when beers were poured,

and on a feast we gorged,

friends we were all,

and then, down from the sky,

the big fireball came,

it took us all, burned us all away,

a fiery cataclysm,

I remember the crazies called it *Judgment Day*!

I remember that night,

when we danced with orgy whores,

and in the flesh, our pleasure surged,

fornicators we were all,

until in flames, our asses raped,

by the big fireball,

and then the big god came down,

and his angels they sang,

on this...on Judgment Day,

that big god selected his chosen,

like a old man at a Chinese buffet,

takes what he wants, what's appetizing,

and sends the rest of us, the damned, away.

And when we got there,

the big devil lit a cigarette,

and took a look around,

"What a waste, these bunch of clowns!

Bring in the hell-hounds!"

The three-headed dogs, to chew us up,

then shit us all away,

then the rain clouds on earth they parted,

clear away the clouds, let the rays of light shine down,

the big fireball was only a rouse,

to bulldozer the old life away,

that bastard god ruined our party,

all for the glorification of his massive ego!

All this just to bring a new world,

a new people,

into a new day,

but we won't forget,

our bodies will rise from the grave,

like the whores we used to dance with,

we will have our second-coming!

Germ

†

The sirens holler, echoes in the skies,

an air raid warning, the screams and cries,

upon the earth below, wallow in sorrow,

their mission is clear, they guard the payload.

Warfare above, as machineguns and bombers,

collide with explosions, twisted metal and charred erosion,

fire spills out, the polluted rain falls,

as torn and pulverized corpses,

drip down from the clouds.

Soldiers scatter civilians below,

a puzzle broken, scattered bones and pieces,

of flesh and oceans of blue turn to blood,

rivers of tears flow, sweat and ashes,

prevent new growth, as viral winds blow.

Vaccination in effect, upon a world that's wrecked,

the sirens blare, the virus flares up a population of rash,

as radiation infects, a new mutation stands erect,

catastrophic events are in effect,

no more cure, humanity is terminal and sick.

The final absolution,

decree from higher authority,

the solution to kill the germ below,

the grand exit of humanity.

The germ has infected!

The germ has spread!

The germ is cantankerous!

The germ is hazardous!

And now,

it has been decided,

the germ must be disposed of!

The final absolution,

decree from higher authority,

the solution to kill the germ below,

the grand exit of humanity.

They hear the leviathan approach,

motors roaring, smog-ridden exhaust corrodes,

and sludge seeps down upon the fleeing germs below!

The final absolution,

decree from higher authority,

the solution to kill the germ below,

the grand exit of humanity.

The people raise their brows,

heads held up to the sky...

"Hail Mary full of grace," a lone whisper utters.

Voices cry in praise for a better place!

"...deliver us from flesh, we who have infected,

take our pollution...dispose of our corrosion,

dispose of our race!" And the whisper, dissipates.

Eyes watch in horror, and they listen,

that horrible shrill, the falling scream.

The final absolution,

decree from higher authority,

the solution to kill the germ below,

the grand exit of humanity.

And then.....it's released,
"whistle while you work, scream while you run!"
as the wail gets closer, heading towards earth,
impact is imminent, as the finger of god,
collides with the ground.

5...4...3...2...1.../\/\/\/\/\/\/\/\/\/\/\/_____

Obliteration,
the virus dissipates,
oceans of red revert to blue,
the flare-ups and rashes have settled,
eons of silence revolve around the sun,
another epoch gone, another epoch to come,
the hot air becomes cool and comfortable,
the world is purified, the water is drinkable.

So it seems,
the solution worked so well,
infected soil heals with time,
all the side-effects subside,

all the germs have died.

The final cure,

leaves the earth lifeless and pure,

no more diseases and plagues to endure,

until, a new strain mutates,

when a new germ evolves to pollinate.

The final absolution,

decree from higher authority,

the solution has killed the germ below,

no more will there be a humanity.

Bloodožer

†

The pale face illuminates

the skeletal remains litter the dirt,

within the headlights,

as the ivory hand of sickle-wielder,

turns the key to ignite,

the rusty shafts and pistons screech,

the gas-tank stomach,

of blood-dozer roars,

the shovel-headed death machine,

it's creaking, metal bones grind,

as over the horizon,

blood-dozer's roar can be heard,

to scrape up the last, the remains of war,

treads crush skulls, obliterate rib cages,

to plow the remains away.

Blood-dozer scrapes up,

with dirt and gravel,

all the flesh and bones,

of human rabble.

The skinless lips of sickle-wielder smile,

as he sops up all the blood,

cleans up all the remains,

the trail of bodies for miles and miles,

to be placed in garbage bags,

tied tight and tossed into the pile,

of mountains to be found,

mountains to be discovered,

to serve as a reminder,

of the mistakes we made,

that cost us our existence forever.

Blood-dozer scrapes up,

with dirt and gravel,

all the flesh and bones,

of human rabble.

Blood-dozer shovels all humanity away!

The job is done,

and sickle-wielder turns the key,

shutting off the genocide machine,

the job is done, a sigh of relief,

"How to spend the rest of eternity?"

Sickle-wielder spreads his wings,

and flies away,

to another planet,

another solar-system,

the universe awaits,

the next path Death with take,

where another machine awaits,

to do its job,

remove the pollution from the universe,

where does the road of eternity lead,

which path will Death take,

parked upon the surface of another ruined planet,

another blood-dozer awaits.

O`paqalypse
†

When there's a scent of mud,

the floods are coming,

the taste of dirt, the water's rising.

The smell of blood,

murder's brewing,

civilization's failing, empire's crumbling.

Blind eyes nothing more than black pits,

seers of the coming cataclysm,

as we are soon to be swallowed,

join the lost planets into the abyss.

Attack, break the necks,

chop the limbs away from the weak,

let them drown, let them be taken away,

retaliate to keep afloat, deicide's rising.

These are not the darkest days,

for the shadows loom nearby on the horizon,

the best of the worst is still to come.

This overflow is getting worse,

and when it all ceases, all the spoils are wasted,

the hunger of the many turns to famine,

cannibalism is the road to self-genocide.

Eat away the remains of lifetimes,

toss away the bones, remains of life-long strife,

bite and tear the meat like rabid dogs,

no more order for the world of disorder.

Be prepared for the worst,

your children, their children, will eat that of you,

which still remains,

for they will have nothing left for themselves.

Remember the warnings and the signs,

be ready for the darkest of days,

your offspring are going to live by instinct,

and keep off the streets at night.

The hunters and the cannibals,

will be prowling the streets,

the blood lust churns in their guts,

searching for the hiding sheep.

The best of the worst...is yet to come...

The Steeple (Intro)

†

Here's the house,

baptized sanctum of the people,

upon its blood-soaked crest,

the diadem, the steeple,

as time moves forward,

and we become a thinking people,

the doors will open,

and there will be no people…

A Haunting in the Chapel

†

I hear their voices,

the echoes and the hymns,

haunting imagery of crucifixion,

stained glass of false prophecy,

written lies and speeches contorted.

Whispers from the podium,

utterance of some ill-belief,

that *"All who do not bask in His glory—*

shall suffer in the fire for eternity!"

These words and images fill me with dread,

by these ghosts of lunatics that try to fill my head,

with their ancient books and holy words,

haunting a place stained in slaughtered hordes.

Chapel of Fools
†

We open our gates, and welcome you in,

leave all worldly possessions,

they're no longer needed, they are a sin,

take their hand and let the ceremonies begin.

And hold a service, and say a prayer,

Don't you know...god is everywhere.

Prophets just they make their speech,

chosen arisen, lift their followers off their feet,

ascend to a higher place by the golden hand,

give the desperate their promised land.

And hold a gathering where all meet,

a final whisper before they sleep.

Seduce the weak of their mortal coil,

stain what hope they had in life, take away free will,

"Everything human must be forsaken,

including the human body, before one can ascend,

this is the last chance to leave earth,

before it's recycled!"

The words of prophets and saviors burn,

from their mouth it drips like acid,

they bite, and from their fangs,

they inject into our blood the poison.

These are the words of prophets,

they feed their followers from filthy hands.

They ate the flesh, they drank the blood,

they swallowed whole and paid the final price.

To exit this world and find a paradise,

this was their final sacrifice.

"How very much I have loved you,

how very much I have tried my best,

to give you the good life.

No man takes my life from me, I lay my life down."

The restless, the wanderers, now let them sleep,

let them drift to where souls may meet,

to see those loving faces in a better land,

guided by spacecraft or by god's hand.

Inject the death where life once dwelled,

force these people from their living hell.

"My heart was crushed to think,

that I led so many people astray.

I was appalled that I could have been so wrong,

and I was deeply grateful that God,

had not struck me dead as a false prophet!"

Fire blazes over, the cleansing process has begun,

false words crushed under rationalized wits,

feed the false ones into the belly of the beast,

where revenge is delivered, by those they deceived!

"Hurry, hurry my children,

No more pain now, no more pain,

All we're doing is laying down our lives."

And the music plays on,

the voices sing in choir,

church bells ring on this final hour.

"All they do is taking a drink,

They take it to go to sleep.

That's what death is, sleep.

You can have it (inaudible) I'm tired of it all."

And the music plays on,

the organs echo louder,

church bells ring, this is the final hour.

"Don't, don't fail to follow my advice,

you'll be sorry, you'll be sorry,

have trust. You have to step across.

Can't some people assure these children,

of the relaxation of stepping over to the next plane?"

Applause fades to silence,

as they take their fate in hand,

they followed like sheep,

parents and their children will forever sleep.

A voice whispers peacefully, *"Take Some..."*

"Take our life from us, we laid it down,

we got tired, we didn't commit suicide,

we committed an act of revolutionary suicide,

protesting the conditions of an inhumane world."

And the music fades,

the crying smothers to silence,

no more speeches, no more promises.

These white nights, now perish into black.

Those who walked into the chapel,

are never coming back.

Be the Believing

†

Spread over the mountains,

and I will soar through the clouds and the misty haze,

it was unclear to me in life, upon this plane,

where I was going, where I am,

but in this death, let the fates take me,

burn me down willingly,

take my body and burn the flesh away,

break me, the brittle statue that I am,

and I will then exist eternally,

upon this world, in this existence,

I will be many, once a skeleton of one,

now the ashes of gods, now the specters of many,

wear the cloak of haze, seer over moons and eons,

walker of the time,

a new god, a new fad, a new divinity,

worship me in the temple of infinity,

bow to the ash,

kneel to the divine,

pray for my blessing,

the ability to walk over seas,

sleep among the restless,

wisp among the trees,

whisper to your thoughts,

scold your insolence,

I am a new being,

I am, for I shall be, the all seeing,

be the believing, believe my deceiving.

A Hungry Deity

†

There's nothing more to say,

once you eat it all away,

all quiet up there today,

what's the matter? You looking down?

Is there nothing you have to say?

There's nothing more to take,

when you threw it all away,

abandonment was your way,

is this your solution? Absolution?

Lost up there in all your delusion?

There's nothing else to make,

you created it all anyway,

just to be destroyed, to be decimated,

was this the grand plan? Are thou still supreme?

Was this all just a part of your scheme?

Created in thy image,

beings that crave more and more,

a hunger never satisfied, and left a full plate,

is it to all go to waste? Is there ever a good taste?

What is the meaning of all this anyway?

Is this what we're supposed to be?!

Malicious, cruel, selfish animals?!

Hypocrites, criminals, deceiving human beings?!

After all, we're the children, of a greedy,

conniving, hungry deity!

"I give you life, now sacrifice it all away!

I give you breath, now you will cease to breathe!

I give you love, sanctity does not pertain to me!

You all belong to me...my pathetic human beings!

Get on your knees and bow, praise me, bleed for me!

Your soul, your family, your life, your possessions,

feed me all you own, your body and mind...feed me...

I'm never full...feed me...all of humankind!

All that's left, you thought was yours...

your hopes and dreams...are mine"

A Part of Something Larger
†

Stone by stone,

a civilization built on backs of slave-labor,

forms an empire, where flows blood of rivers,

into chalices where the strong,

drink the life of the weak,

drip by drip,

the blood of billions, flows into the ocean,

of something larger, something greater,

something worse...something better?

Brick by brick,

these slaves of humankind,

serve their gods, worship their deities,

and brick by brick, they build their towns,

they construct their cities,

monuments meant to last infinitely,

to be a part of something larger.

Prayer by prayer,

order after order,

sacrifice the blood of animals,

sacrifice the strength of man,

sacrifice the flesh of all,

and leaders become gods, gods become titans,

cannot be touched, cannot be seen,

living in castles, in churches, in skyscrapers,

in cathedrals, in synagogues, in mosques,

lavish robes or business attire,

human kings, human leaders,

a higher aristocracy inherited at birth,

to reign for hours, for days, for months, for years,

to reign forever, to ascend above mortals,

to ascend beyond time, ascend beyond space,

and all the universe is rearranged, reorganized,

reevaluated...a natural order, of nature no longer,

under divine men, callus and without honor.

Stone by stone,

up from the natural earth,

a phoenix from ashes reprises,

a flameless burning, as the torch of nature,

will take a foothold, and her kingdom,

will grow again and a natural order,

will be reestablished, and this divine catastrophe,

will fall and be divine no longer,

as civilizations begin to fall, as time takes hold,

and the tendrils twist, the tendrils pull,

structures down and crushes brick into rubble,

towers into rock, as spires begin to crumble,

to renew nature, to rid the world of man-made power,

forever, and no longer,

will we sacrifice the blood of animals,

no longer will we sacrifice the strength of man,

no longer will flesh be scarred and bled,

by building an infrastructure,

for these role-playing men,

in lavish robes and business attire.

And natural order, will be restored,

to be renewed, to live forever,

rocks and rivers, upon which branches will sail,

flora and fauna of a vast, abundant kind,

will have their own simple tale to tell,

all part of a round table, headed by evolution,

presided over by the healing hands of nature,

a long, ageless, ancient order,

descendants of air and elements, seeds and flowers,

living organisms, who lived a peaceful existence,

before the coming of man...and civilization,

to disrupt and destroy the natural order,

a natural order predating myself and all mankind,

a natural order...that deserves back what we have taken,

a natural order, to live on forever...

Goathead

†

There was an execution today,

a man hanged, for crimes against all humanity,

at the rim beyond the state line,

upon the mountain tops, against a blood-red sky,

at the summit of Goat's Head,

where all the evil men die.

And, some say,

stay out too long, hang around long enough,

and the devil comes in the dead of night,

an old man, with lantern in hand,

hoofed feet, and his face...well,

people described this cloaked man,

as an urban legend, with a goat's head...

Pillar of Thorns

†

Another sacrifice is made,

as demons in the sky drag the damned below,

toss the bodies like rag dolls,

across blood red skies,

to be impaled, on the thorns below,

upon pillars of burning crimson,

stained with the stench of death,

of not the millions of lives taken,

but rather, by those who cause war, murder, famine,

impaled upon metal and razor-headed stakes.

Blood rises in the oceans red below,

where tiny ships of coffins sail and flow,

as blood within the coffins swells,

and the raging claws and talons, tentacles and jaws,

of meat-eaters break open the shell to drink the yolk,

the bloated soul within, for this damned monster,

and for all their atrocities, hell has come,

and that eternal rest, is forever disturbed.

Punctured for their atrocities, by acid-stained swords,

as the demons carry the new arrivals,

up and up, higher and higher, to be released,

and join the wretched,

to be impaled upon the pillar of thorns!

Pentagram

†

Five disciples, stand before seven thrones,

five disciples each, sacrifice their soul,

to seven demons, seven lords of desolation.

Four gateways open,

four cardinals each without discretion,

the robes and hats of red burn, the four gateways open,

the doors close behind, the red feathers burn,

north, south, east, and west, all are lost,

none shall be hallow, none shall lay to rest.

Three victims of fate, three O faithful,

the father, the son, and the holy ghost, shall be no more,

no more rebirth, no more protection,

as the ashes spread of their reverse crucifixion,

across their brow as they bow their heads.

Two artifacts, the black dagger and the red candle wax,

alight the altar, spill the blood of this sacrifice,

reborn unto the world, the titan O the atronach,

the spawn of thunder, the spawn of twisters,

the eyes of the restless, the horrors of the nightmares,

bound to this sleeplessness.

One master, one rules over all, one to spurn the world,

one master, so do as your told,

as he pours the chalice, tips the scales,

and the world is covered in darkness,

when life ceases, all eager listeners fall to the silence,

one master to play god,

one snags the chains of his dogs,

one to summon his demons upon earth, one to many,

and many to drag them down,

one rules among seven,

the beast and his realm of hell,

the betrayer, the desecrater, once the light-bearer,

once a star shining amongst the heavens.

wanting to keep things clean,

they worship in ancient buildings, wanting to be clean,

but they have forgotten what this all once meant,

born of ignorance and it has spread,

this is a different world from the once pristine,

now this world I see…is…obscene…

7 Kings

†

Lucifer.....

Once a celestial light,

the betrayer of God,

has fallen from the heavens!

Beelzebub.....

A swarm of jealousy,

pride eats from a decrepit hand,

oh lord of the flies!

Sathanus.....

Deceiver upon mankind,

malevolent entity of wrath,

eternal war end of days!

Abaddon.....

Destroyer never satisfied,

to pave the way of all men,

into a bottomless pit!

Mammon.....

125

Gleaming gates of gold,

lead thy soul into possession,

where moth and dust corrupt!

Belphegor.....

His reign falls from April skies,

as intelligence desires invention,

and twists convention into corruption!

Asmodeus.....

King nine, Lord of the seven,

love a conscript for corrosion,

passion secretes sludge!

Prince of Darkness

†

There's been a breach,

a crack in the situation,

the season is changing,

a solstice in motion.

Steam a putrid stench,

emitting from the earth's pores,

geysers rupture, pressure boils over,

hell's coming and close behind,

annihilation with it,

the seal's been broken,

the four-horseman ride.

Soul's of the departed,

drift for eternity, aimless,

no longer can they hear the angel's song,

as before them, gate's of gold,

open into charred halls,

from within the fortress,

the prince of darkness calls.

Bells chime upon the witching hour,

his grasp upon their souls,

the paralyzing touch of black fingers,

cannot be removed.

Paint the Horses Apocalypse

†

The fear, the mayhem,

the ripping and tearing to ensue,

four horsemen of pain,

ready to carry out thy doom.

Crosses burning, as the guilty one is led,

into the center of the crowd,

and the angel of death looms above,

string up the arms, string up the legs,

bound and pulled by heated iron hooks,

to rip the limbs away.

Four directions of pain,

the agony unbearable to believe,

to leave nothing left, but a quivering head and torso,

like an insect, the limbs ripped away.

Paint the horse of agony a yellow tint,

paint the horse of sickness a horrid green,

paint the horse of execution a bloody red,

and the horse of death,

black as ash with the crow's wings!

Horses pull in all directions, and the tendons rip away,

leaving a screaming, dying man,

wishing death would come faster to him on this day,

but the horses don't go far enough,

and the screaming man must wait,

as the men bring the knives,

and cut the rest of him away.....

I Am Many

†

A man shattered, a man torn,

arises from the catacombs,

to test his fate, to exhume what's beneath,

to face the lion of Judah, the prince,

who upon his brow wears the crown of thorns.

Upon this man's arms, are the cuts and tears,

where he would rip away his flesh with stone,

to bleed the visions of demons from tainted nights,

he would scream, he would cry, wail and whine,

he could not be bound, he could not be tied.

And the lion raises his hands,

the prince demands the evil spirit subside,

"What do you want with me Jesus,

oh mighty son of God?!

We won't go back, not there! You dare not torment us!"

"Tell me your name...confess to me your disguise!"

The man writhes, as inside,

this thing twists within his flesh,

his eyes burned by the savior's light,

the light of the heavens, the light of redemption.

The demon within shows through,

as the theologian watches this man's face contort,

weeping in pain and agony from eternal misery,

he screams with daemonic fervor and rage,

as echoes of puke and bile reach out to say:

"I am many...we won't go back, don't send us away!"

And the lion steps forward, raises his hands,

he grips the spirits within with the strength of faith,

the shades within are trepidated,

cast out through his mouth, exorcised away,

and the man, worn and beaten, falls to his knees,

watching the light chase the nightmares away.

Fed to the pigs,

the shepherds herd them by the thousands,

and lead them to the mouth of rivers,

to be swallowed away, drowned beneath the oceans,

132

where beneath the waves, these demons will stay.

The savior holds out his hand,

and helps this man to his feet.

"Give this man some clothes, feed him, let him sleep.

What final judgment awaits the others...we shall see."

Bloodworks

†

High above in the majestic heavens,

where mighty citadels of gold and ivory stand,

wages a civil war of gods and angels,

an eternal battle since the ancient days.

There can only be one god,

there can only be one...higher power!

Flaming swords and golden armor,

crash and strike against the defending forces,

the siege upon god's realm has been waged,

as one angel stands among the others, his fist raised.

There can only be one god,

there can only be one higher power,

as Lucifer and his rebels,

fight against the forces of Michael!

And with a final stand, Lucifer looks out over the horizon,

he cries for war and the angels soar in battalions,

Michael stands to bring the Light-Bearer down,

and with god's command, the fallen angels are cast out.

There can only be one god,

there can only be one higher power,

as Michael and his arch-angels,

cast the betrayers out, and blood skies rain with fire!

The gladiatorial war, the bloodbath of angels ceases,

as it shall take eons to wash the ivory lands clean,

for down below, the bloodworks await,

as screaming angels fall to earth.

The betrayers, the loss of Paradise,

shall thunder in the skies forever,

as the blood flows over when the clouds part,

and empties below into the lake of fire!

Pass the Final Judgment

†

Awaiting the final punishment,

at the edge of the universe,

before the thrones of immortality,

at their backs the palaces of ivory arise,

and at the pinnacle, the Prince of Lions sits,

beneath his altar, at his pristine feet,

millions of the lost and meek, fall and praise his name,

this idol of benediction, this idol of fame,

this judge of saints and sinners, prisoners on the lame.

The wretch before me walks upon the clear marble sky,

and the judge looks down with wide and glaring eyes:

"Mortal man...I smell your blood, for it has spoiled,

I see into your flesh,

for your wicked ways are transparent,

I know your thoughts, they are forbidden,

I cast out your soul from paradise!"

The skies part, and he falls away,

into a realm of fire and flame.

And now I proceed,

before the judge of hell and heaven,

for whom my fate is in this deity's hands,

and my soul, is for fate to keep,

he looks at me, sighs, then proceeds to speak:

"You...your blood boils,

and your mind is thick and muddled,

you have thoughts of sadness, thoughts of grandeur,

thoughts of anger, thoughts of splendor,

jealousy and bitterness, you feel pity,

yet preach hostility and no regret."

"Your nothing but a hypocrite,

your destruction...you burned,

all the bridges of those you met,

and they move on, while you're stuck behind,

what to do...when I look at all of you,

what am I to do with your kind?!"

He pondered for a moment, then made his choice,

he spoke to the masses, and to myself,

in that roaring, thundering voice:

"You seemed an honest fellow,

a hard worker through and through,

but I feel you've given up,

there's no place in there for you.

This is a place for those who are ready to move on,

those who have seen the light,

they've left their worldly possessions,

their malice, anger, cruelty, plights,

all their emotions behind,

they have no regrets, their ready to move on,

but for you...I fear,

the time has come...."

"I pass my final judgment,

and cast you below,

for there is no coming back,

your judgment...to hell you go!"

The clouds part, I feel the fires rise,

as the earth beneath me opens wide,

no coming back, no release from the demon's hold,

and it's from now, until eternity to go...

Paradise or Inferno

†

What's it gonna be then eh?

heaven...maybe hell,

paradise and salvation,

or into the inferno of damnation,

is there right, or is it all wrong?

To rise above or fall below,

soar along with the shaping of the clouds,

or sink into the earth,

as they lay buried like stones underground,

no salvation or motivation can be found.

The breeze is cool and the mantle warm,

the banner of the seasons rise and fall,

a new identity for what is right, is wrong,

a war of voices, voices of war,

elation and isolation, we've seen it all before.

The positives become the negatives,

opposites think they attract,

one minute your hot and then your burned,

stand to long and your frozen in time,

I've seen the entire map,

and the grass is dead on both sides.

Let them be original,

let them blend in to the scenes,

let the individual do the talking,

and the choices suit the physiological needs,

serve and love in blessed gardens,

or manage the down-trodden forever.

So what's it gonna be?

To lead the way or fall behind,

the king becomes the emperor,

the servants and slaves are left to suffer,

but the knights have abandoned their round-table,

and the peasants take their place.

Who will run the show,

who's been doing what, do we really know,

who will rule and who will follow,

what's next on the bucket list for tomorrow?

Is there a better place we can all go?

Or are we trapped, forced to exist in this inferno?

The Final Descent

†

Lost within my nightmares,

I awaken...I look about into the dismal fog,

and I wonder...who is this shade,

this shadow that stands before me?

He holds out his hand, and lifts me to my feet,

he smiles...though more like a grimace of pain,

he speaks softly, though sincere in meaning.

"You must come with me now! For this nightmare,

it only gets worse. A macabre tale,

that is your own doing."

"Who...who are you? You look so familiar, but it's hard,

it's hard to remember."

"You know my face, my words, my voice,

from long lost days of yore...my name...is Daniel Gerry,

and it's time."

"Time for what?" I ask, my thoughts tremble,

at this man's poetic way of speaking.

"It's time...to make your final descent...time to face,

the depths of Hell once more!"

"Hell? What madness is this? Who are you really?!"

"Inferno was my creation...my lost faith,

to God's bidding, my cowardice and all my sins,

I've made my journey...atoned for lost divinity...

for I...you would-be poet! I am Dante Alighieri!

But you, what they call...American...you will call me,

Daniel Gerry.

Your Hell...your Anger! Is only the beginning!

of what atrocities, are waiting..."

To Hell I Go

†

-The Surface-

The Desolate City

The wind of sorrow and the rain of pain,

lash day and night in this desolate place,

what's that sound I hear which echoes behind walls,

but the cries of the dead,

as they rise from the cracks and crevices,

of their decayed shells and mortal coils,

they traverse down the stairs,

and stand before ten-thousand thrones of gold,

the greedy reach, but the whips of the guardians,

keep them back and in check,

one half-man, a horse and a bull for its head,

the other a woman wearing a tiara of snakes,

in single-file, the herds descend,

to be judged by the kings at the gates of the dead.

"Let us follow...and see what fate awaits for them..."

Kings at Judgment

The kings bicker amongst themselves,

deciding where these abominations should go,

deciding what damnation lies ahead,

decisions, decisions, decisions,

and no time to rest, no time to wait,

there's horrible phantoms to be seen to here,

even if it takes all eternity...oh wait....

At the center is seated a judge in black,

powdered wig and all,

he breaks apart the monotony,

silences the shrilling echoes within these halls.

He smells the air and snorts in agony,

the first in line has lived his whole life in gluttony,

"So it shall be, by the power invested in me!

You there! To the Chamber of Pounding!"

And into the black he goes, whimpering, moaning,

as he steps on down the jet-black road.

Next in line, the crying soul steps forward,

and like before, amongst the arguing kings,

the judge sniffs the air and retorts,

this one is of greed, and has coerced,

the stench of the poor and hard-working is on his hands,

"So it shall be, by the power invested in me!

You greedy bastard, you take from others,

the Mountain of Knives, you will climb!"

And into the black, he howls as he crawls,

the guardians boot him in the ass as he stumbles along.

The next soul drenches her naked body,

in tears of depraved regret and insanity,

and the judge sniffs the air, horrified...

by this monster's heinous crime!

"So it shall be, by the power invested in me!

Despicable woman! Vile bitch!

Abandoned your newborn, let him drown in water!"

The woman cries and pleas,

"I am sorry for what I've done...please, please!

Forgive me, I...I was not ready...!"

He gurgles the rage and swallows hard,

all the punishment she shall endure,

all the pain she will feel, she will suffer,

he bangs the gavel upon the marble altar.

"Abandoning and killing a newborn!

For that, you will go to the lower levels,

where you will hold rocks,

a thousand times your weight,

and just before your bones snap under pressure,

you will fall...you will drown in a putrid lake!"

He falls to a whisper,

"The responsibility of that child was yours,

and you failed him, for that there is no forgiveness,

the light is closed to you...let the darkness rape you!"

She will not budge, she refuses to go,

wanting, pleading to hold her child once more,

the guardian of serpents,

and the guardian of multi-faces,

grips her by the arms,

and tosses her in, to where exists,

these abysmal places.

Daniel grasps me by the arm, as I watch in horror,

as these tortured shapes are wrangled along,

I turn to him, and he says to me,

"This way, I want to show you something,

before we proceed."

View from the Tower

He leads me across the crumbled ruins,

and before us stands tilted, a spiral stair,

leading up, and we ascend,

towards the pinnacle of this altered tower.

We look across canyons and planes,

only the upper-level is visible,

crumbled domes keep from view,

the horrors of the lower levels.

Across the skies of dried winds and pale spheres,

we watch these tortured spirits,

slip among their trail of tears,

from up here, we see all that is and to be.

As they cross the bridge into the abyss,

where all lost souls shall remain for eternity.

"This is just the beginning,

for what is to come to pass,

as we descend further,

that is where we'll see, where we'll find,

were we'll walk among the damned of all time..."

"And, these places..." I ask with a shudder,
"The pounding, the mountain of knives...?"

He closes his eyes, silent for a moment,
he sighs, then turns to me,
"You'll see it all, the torture and the misery,
you'll see it all...you will see..."

Divine Orders

We descend the stairs of the damned,

and stand before the judge in the powdered wig,

he sniffs the air, and notices something different,

"I smell flesh, I hear the blood in your veins,

this is no place for the living, come back,

and when your rotting soul stands before me,

I'll decree where you deserve to go!"

He slams the gavel, and the guardians step forward.

"Now just hold on! I am here on divine orders!"

Daniel cries, and from his crimson robes,

hands the guardians the rolled piece of paper.

The guardian of snakes, hands the paper to the judge,

who grasps the parchment with animosity,

"This is a waste of my time,

how dare you bother me with these..."

He reads the words listed,

where was this paper? I must have missed it.

The judge mumbles as he scrolls along,

he looks up at Daniel and then to me,

hands the paper back and slams the gavel,

"So, I see...very well...guardians open the gates,

and let these two proceed!"

As we pass by, he stops me,

"I warn you mortal...you won't like what you see!"

He laughs, and Daniel and I move along.

Together we stand before,

a huge black tunnel and along the outside,

an altered portal carved from slabs of black marble,

where etched in stone, the chilling words...

"Abandon all hope, ye who enter here..."

Daniel stops before we enter.

"I remember these words,

I remember them well,

this is the pinnacle,

before we descend into undying hell..."

Bridge of Helplessness

Before our steps,

stands the infernal bridge,

where beneath our feet,

there is nothing but an empty abyss.

"A pit as empty as these souls,

here is where they cast away all hopes,

all light is offered into these pools of black,

this is it for them, for they are never coming back..."

We stride along, past sullen faces,

heads to the ground,

their minds lost to time,

by fate and past disgraces.

Then one looks up, and he speaks to me,

he grasps my arm and pulls me in,

"Are you here to help?! Help me...help me please!"

He rushes to the edge,

of the helpless bridge,

and jumps, takes the final leap,

only to be rematerialized,

and now his gaze upon me is gone,

whatever was left, has now been left behind.

Others follow, raining bodies fall,

plummeting to the abyss below,

they return, they're brought back,

now only shells of what they once were.

"The abyss doesn't take everything,

it leaves one thought, one memory,

their crimes, their sins in life,

it will replay in their thoughts,

over and over for all eternity..."

I could only reply, *"My anger and my hurtful thoughts,*

they're not worth this insanity!"

"Insanity? You are not here,

for your mental clarity to be questioned.

This isn't a place to be driven insane,

for if that is what you take from all this,

then our quest will be in vane!"

"Then why must I be forced,

to see such awful sights! Such awful treatment?"

He sighs. *"Then you missed the point,*

these souls are here of their own doing,

nothing more, it's too late for them,

but you have been given another chance..."

"A chance for what? To better myself,

I'm better let's go back, I've seen enough!"

We reach the end of the bridge,

and stand before another door,

where inside roars thunder and,

and the winds rattle the hinges.

"No you haven't,

I must be sure, as someone who,

has chosen anger instead of love,

jealousy instead of accepting what is,

hostility towards others, instead of forgiving,

isolation...instead of living.

There is more for you to see,

156

death is not the same as life,

a living soul can learn, can change,

while death is permanent, and there is no going back.

Consider this, as another point of view,

seeing things on the other side,

your actions must be different,

or else you'll wind up here for all time.

So, I ask you...will you proceed,

and gain knowledge, learn from another's mistakes,

see that things can be far worse?

Or will you remain ignorant and stubborn as you are,

be no different, and seal your doom?"

I watch the billions leap from this bridge,

as the darkness below swallows them whole,

watch them lumber along,

to where their paths go,

mindless and empty, cursing all they've done,

"I'm not like them," I say. *"Let's move on..."*

"Beyond this door,

is the first step into hell,

the first layer is of Wind and Thunder,

where those who steal for greed dwell..."

"Greed is a common trait,

amongst all mortals. They covet,

and they steal, they want what others have,

they want what they can't get,

what they cannot attain for themselves,

they wait for others to gain,

and that's when these vultures take..."

"And after that, then what?" I ask.

"You shall see, for the eighteen layers await..."
He states.

"Eighteen?! I thought there were nine?" I reply.

He laughs, *"People have become more creative,*
in their crimes since my time..."

-The Outer Level-

Northern Corridor:
The Greed of Thieves and Gluttons

The Chamber of Wind and Thunder
-

We pass beyond the doors,

to where storms and silver rain, howl with fury,

this is the chamber of wind and thunder,

watch as the guilty attempt to flee and scurry.

Confronted by mountains of gold and diamonds,

but the thieves cannot take,

constantly barraged by a wind of coins,

their flesh pelted by all they stole in life.

The more they stole, the thicker the wind,

their flesh forever stings by the coins and chalices,

diamonds and rubies that swell the skin,

a thousand times worse than hale or a bee sting.

"Stand back, or the projectiles will attack you too!

Don't get too close, or the winds will bloody you!"

Daniel points over to the far walls of the chasm,

upon the mighty bell towers,

are tied the tortured souls,

whenever they think of money,

the huge bells toll.

The thundering roar,

will forever drive them insane,

they can never break their binds,

they can never get away.

"Wealth is all that is on their minds,

those bells will ring forever,

for all eternity, beyond the span of time!"

We rummage across the gold-plated floor,

until we come to the next chamber door,

I hurry to open it, but the latch is molten,

Daniel says, *"Allow me...",*

and we avoid the storms and hurry in.

Before us lays, a vast and wide mountain range,

where the combustion of smoke and fire dwells,

volcanoes as high as the ceilings,

where upon the lava-tipped crest,

the cheaters and sore-losers,

shove each other in.

"Look at them,

too afraid to lose so they sacrifice each other,

not aware that everyone at some point,

has to feel the burn of failure..."

Scrambling in a sea of elbows and arms,

they flail fists and bite and shove the other,

another falls, as they incinerate in flames,

then another, and another and another.

Their remains flow down a molten river,

where they are gathered into a pile of ashes.

Here a guardian with a gasmask and shovel,

scoops them up and sorts out the pieces,

and the ashes rematerialize,

to be hauled up by a cart to the craters,

and they will cheat and shove all over again.

Daniel looks at me,

"Cheaters...they never learn, do they?"

The Mountain of Knives

We continue along the mountain range,

and upon our shoulders,

starts to fall an ice-cold rain,

the rain smells acrid, the rain smells of poison,

the spoiled blood of the wailing souls,

drips down from the blades of that mountain.

Horror stings me, a sight I have never seen,

a terror fills me, I look away I cannot bear it,

a single mountain rises before us,

upon its peaks, where should be rocks and cliffs,

are razor blades and jagged staves,

...and...where there should be trees,

are the quivering bodies of impaled beings,

they wiggle and squirm, stuck like pigs,

wailing as they attempt to move,

their arms raised upwards!

I stop, and Daniel grips me,

"We have to go further,

that is where our path leads!"

"That..." I gag, *"Is that the mountain of knives?!"*

He nods, *"Those are the many who took advantage,*

of others charities and weakness,

those who took by force from others,

those who coerced and those who were conniving..."

"They're stuck there! Where do they think they're going?

And that screaming! That horrible yelling!"

I cover my ears, I cannot stand it!

He points, *"Up there, at the top,*

is the pinnacle of forgiveness and the promise,

to be redeemed, but they don't realize,

now they are the ones who are being slighted,

they are the ones who are being deceived!"

"The greed of these men and women,

it will bleed and run all over these caverns,

eventually causing it to flood,

and they will drown in the pool of wealth and power,

that they created, see..."

164

And he points to the ground, where the blood is rising,

the cracks in the floor are filling,

"We better keep moving..."

We navigate our way through the nooks and valleys,

following the flock of vultures that hover,

taking bits and chunks out of the bodies,

of the restless stuck upon these ledges of knives.

"Follow the birds, they know which way to go!"

And the flocks lead us forward through this maze,

seas of jagged spires and sharpened spades,

I look up once more,

a last look at this horrific juggernaut before we depart,

and there, struggling near the base,

of the gleaming steel and iron,

riveted to planks by corroded bolts,

is that corrupt who cheated,

his employees, clients, and countless others,

and gained more for himself than deserved.

He writhes and struggles,

with every move, he screams in agony and pain,

he looks familiar, but I cannot place his name,

his features old and decrepit,

rotten by the guilt and the shame,

another carcass, a cloud for this acrid rain.

He looks at me,

blood fills his eyes,

all tears have long dried up.

He looks at me, and with a moan he cries,

"I have left a legacy of shame,

as some of my victims have pointed out,

to my family and my grandchildren.

This is something I am damned with for eternity,

I'm sorry..."

He looks away and tries to continue his climb,

he will go nowhere, here, there is no stock-market,

there are no ranks of financial institution to climb,

only to be stuck to this mountain,

reaching for the ultimate profit he'll never find.

Daniel calls to me,

"This way, there is a place through here..."

The Chamber of Pounding

Over the rim, echoes the grunts and screams,

of the breathless being forced to eat,

we look over and down the hillside,

where many gluttons have been tied,

as guardians big, fat blobs of warts and folds,

stuff their hellish concoctions,

into the mouths of the full.

The guardians dip large wooden spoons,

into a boiling cauldron of a brown and yellow,

bile of sludge and goop.

"Eat it! Don't you dare waste it!"

One of the guardian's screams,

forcing some awful puss-looking mush,

into the mouth of the victim bound to his seat.

"Keep to the shadows, we don't want to be seen,

unless of course...you would like a bite to eat?"

I shook my head no,

"What is that their feeding them anyway?"

I tried to ask without gagging,

and vomiting at the sight of chunky fluid,

being forced down the maw of these souls.

Daniel held his mouth and shook his head,

"You don't want to know..."

"What happens when their full?" I wish I never asked,

he simple pointed and said, *"Try not to gag..."*

A woman was about to burst,

so they untied her and threw her on a table belly up,

she twisted and whined in agony,

her insides cramping up from all the pain,

as her stomach gurgled, and the acid enflames.

They place the table near the cauldron,

one of the fat guardians grabs hold of a massive hammer,

he raises the mallet high, level with her guts,

and with a single blow, her bowels explode,

and into the pot, her residue pours,

they stir it up for the rest to gorge.

"Tie her back up and get her fed,

and grab another tick that needs to be bled!"

I close my eyes and run away,

I can't stand this any longer,

I have to get away.

I curl up beneath a withered tree,

I care not for its purpose of torture and sadistic intent,

I just want to go to sleep,

and wake up from this accursed dream,

I want this nightmare to end...please tell me I'm asleep!

I feel a hand on my shoulder,

startled, I scream,

"Silence, it's only me! We have to move on,

you must follow me!"

"I...I can't, I can go no further!

I want to wake up, and be in this nightmare no longer!"

"This is not a nightmare,

this is your fate if you do not change what is reality,

your attitude stinks! It reeks like that pot of bile,

and with the same bad taste! Now...!"

He holds out his hand to me,

I grab hold and he lifts me up,

he proceeds down the bank a ways,

upon the winds that bellow, his robes kick up,

a crimson sheet that soars in the wind,

where upon his brow rustles the crown of ivy,

"A wannabe poet...we'll see!"

I follow behind, and together,

we trace a thick pool of blood,

before us lies the next layer.

"We stand at the gates stained,

with the blood of the innocent,

the blood of the weak,

and the blood of the helpless,

as within we will find those responsible,

for the cause of so much death..."

Without further ado,

down into the second layer we go...

Western Corridor:
Where the Blood Runs with Slaughter

The Chamber of Stampede

Upon the other side, we hear the thunder,

the snorting and the roar, of bestial devastation,

the screams and cries as souls are trampled underneath,

we open the doors, blood-soaked and stained,

upon the other side of these ancient caverns,

that shake and rattle as hordes of souls are running,

from herds of steeds and oxen.

"Those who harmed animals in life,

their bones are trampled and shattered,

their incorporeal flesh is ripped and mashed,

so they can feel the pain they have caused,

to those creatures without a voice, who were helpless."

I point to the further reaches,

where on the other side,

reside placid lakes and streams,

and these souls look into them,

as though they are waiting.

"What about them...they're just sitting there, waiting?"

Before long, arising up from sterile red seas,

massive snakes and crocodiles of enormous size,

grasp their prey, crunch upon their flesh,

and the serpents and the reptiles,

drag them down into eternal depths.

"They beat and terrorized,

they tormented and tortured,

and into those waters,

those beast will tear them asunder."

Fountains of blood gush up from the waters,

as the pieces and remains of these souls,

float up, heads, arms, legs, guts and intestines,

drift on down an endless current,

these wretched beings,

will never rematerialize,

they will forever linger in the blood of their doing.

Daniel turns and says we must continue on,

"And now...we'll see what happens,

to those that have slaughtered other people..."

The Forest of Blades

Ahead of us, a glimmering forest lays,

"This is where the murderers must tread,

the forest of blades, to forever be bled..."

Off to either side, the red current flows along,

the pieces of the maimed drift on.

But ahead, it's the wailing and the screams,

that catches my attention,

and Daniel tells me, that is where our path leads.

"I know a secret way around, follow me."

We take a secret path, over scorching molten hills,

the burn is harsh beneath my bare feet,

but this is the experience, the pain I must endure,

until we reach our end, the final road to destiny.

Atop the hill, we watch beneath,

as screaming bodies force their way through,

an array of branches and trees,

welded together by fire and metals of the earth,

shaped into a forest of voracious trees,

some of these faces I recognize from life,

these blood thirsty criminals and human beings,

it seems in the end, they got what they deserved,

for their violent acts of discord.

"I know what it is your thinking...is it wise?

To want this pain to be brought upon others,

does it make you feel any better?"

Daniel says, and I know he's right,

my hurtful feelings towards others,

makes me no different than these swine,

but there I go again...I hope I can get better by the end.

Up from these woods of spikes, I can hear them,

as the blades gouge and stab at their skin,

in life, as did they, from up here,

I can hear them speak, and scream the reasons,

for what they did and why.

"I killed for love...my wife and her lover intertwined!"

"I killed out of hate...I detested my brother!"

"I killed for fun...I love to watch as I slaughter!"

176

"I killed out of faith...my disagreement with others,

my faith and theirs were different...and I was chosen,

to make them see the light!"

Their flesh gets ripped upon the spears,

and branches drenched in red,

as that blood collects and runs over,

to flow into the endless river.

I turn to Daniel,

"So, with my thoughts of cold blood,

I sometimes have, tell me enlightened phantom,

is this where I would be?"

He shakes his head,

"No...there is a darker realm,

and to that place we will soon be,

so walk with me unenlightened mortal,

and let us proceed..."

Chamber of Dismemberment

Before us we behold,

a chamber of mutilation and screams,

a menagerie of torture devices and means,

to cause pain to the sadists,

to cause eternal misery to the disdain butchers,

here is where they are ripped apart,

and chopped to pieces.

"Over there, some hang upside down,

as a hack saw tears through their body,

the torturers will rip these souls in half,

separating the bliss they felt by the pain they caused,

and all that will remain...is agony."

"Ahead of us, some will be laid upon stone tables,

upon a sheet of white paper,

and hear that..."

There is the sound of a stone wheel,

sharpening a steel blade.

Over there, next to the table,

hulking men in white aprons stained with blood,

prepare for the dismembering.

"These souls will be butchered into pieces,

then wrapped up in the paper,

they will be packaged and prepared for feasting,

the way they butchered and devoured others in life..."

He points over to a large dining table,

where massive shapes in tuxedoes and dresses sit,

awaiting to eat, waiting to be fed.

"The remains to be used later,

will be hung upon meat hooks within the coolers,

and the rest will be discarded, over there,

additions to the endless river."

I was curious, afraid before, but now I had to ask,

"Where does this river lead?"

He nods ahead of us,

"Ahead...is where you will find your answer at last."

Chamber of Blood

I hear the dripping of this foul water,

as it leaks somewhere into a vast pool,

over beyond the rim we follow,

through a makeshift winding road of valleys,

where from some unspeakable source,

the winds bellow, and that rotting smell,

we must follow.

"You are about to see, the source of the earth,

where the blood of humankind resides..."

And we reach the edge,

a fowl and lifeless shore,

where all rivers run into,

it is here where all time stops,

where the docks of alternate passages rest,

we stand upon the ocean's crest,

upon the shoreline of an ocean of blood,

at the bottom, beneath the gagging waves,

of putrid spoiled blood,

soured by its reasons, curdled for its existence,

far beneath are the billions and billions,

of the slaughtered and the dead, and with them,

are those souls who killed and mutilated,

this is where the remains of their fate stays,

washed over by the seas of their pain and misery,

beneath the blood ocean of infinities.

"This is where the remains go,

pieces and horrors of their past life,

drift along the endless river,

to pour out from the mouth of death,

to be spewed and regurgitated here."

"At the bottom is where they will remain,

to linger and drown in the presence,

of all they have caused pain to,

of all they have taken from life,

to never again reach the surface,

never again to see a ray of light..."

Self-reflection,

and the familiar feeling of drowning,

resonates deep within me,

just to imagine, choking upon this water,

drowning in uncertain fate,

the taste of blood in my mouth,

the thought of blood on my mind,

makes my eyes blacken, and I feel,

consciousness come undone.

I guess realization has a way,

of having its way with a weaker mind,

one not exposed to the horrors of an even worse reality,

there was a moment where my imagination,

my own conjured feelings and ideas,

had the better of me, as the handle upon myself,

vanished from my very being.

I awaken, a familiar feeling and image,

seems to be replaying before my eyes,

not knowing where I am,

and seeing Daniel standing there above me.

It wasn't all just a nightmare after all,

and the reverberations of screams,

echoing through these caverns,

that familiar terror returns to me.

"You're finally awake,
here take my hand."

I stand to my feet.

"Don't let the darkness take you just yet,
we still have a ways to go...and sadly,
the things we'll see from this moment on,
it only gets worse..."

-The Inner Level-

Eastern Corridor:
Castration of Deviance and Molestation

The Chamber of Scissors
-
"Snip...snip...is what we do to the animals,

and down here, it's no different.

Here the screams through that door,

let's venture through and see more..."

I stand before a door, bound in chains,

where inside resides, those who had no control,

the sexually deranged.

The bolts and locks keep them back,

holding down their sexual deviancy,

they could not control in life,

at these gates stand two guardians,

more ferocious and terrifying than the others,

one a sneering jackal draped in black armor,

his claws are fierce, but his eyes and smile,

are creepier.

Next to him, a bestial babe,

crowned in black stags,

eyes seducing and long black tongue,

ensnaring as she throws down her shield,

and her and the jackal,

become entwined with passion,

as we take the key and sneak on by.

"Hold your breath, for in here,

the stench of perversion and lust reeks."

Daniel says to me.

We open the doors, and step inside,

steam is released from this stinking abyss,

where the pain and agony rises up,

from the pits beneath,

stinking, belching anus of the deep.

We walk over hills that moan,

bleed with desire, scream with pleasure,

and upon the other side, resides,

the chamber that separates,

185

the rapists from their members.

"These animals, here they face castration,
an eternal fate to be without sexual gratification,
for children and the weak were their prey,
and now, they'll be cut away..."

He points,

to where these filthy beasts are chained,

as deformed and twisted children,

with scissors and knives for hands,

rise up from the crust of white sands,

to cut and tear their genitals away.

I cannot bear to watch,

as *"they"* are cut and torn away,

and scorching fire from inferno guns,

cauterize in between,

my hands upon my ears, cannot silence the wails,

of those horrific screams.

"Please! Make it stop!
I cannot bear this anymore!"

And all Daniel says to me,

"That is what their victims said,

and nobody could help them,

nobody heard their screams either."

He puts his arm upon my shoulder,

and we move along.

The smell, my god the smell,

the fried sting of meat lingers in the air,

rotten and crisp with every wisp of breath.

I hear the bubbling of cauldrons,

and the crackle of boiling oil,

the gurgles of the drowning,

and the cries for help of flesh searing.

"Observe the pools, of grease and oil,

here the souls are tossed into baskets,

and the guardians dip them in,

where they fry to a crisp.

First they sweat by the memories of their infidelity,

the pressure they feel of being caught,

heightened their ecstasy,

now the guilt turns the dials, of the temperature,

where they will burn for eternity."

Their marriage, their relationships,

lacked the spice and the pleasure,

those souls are taken to giant pots and pans,

to be seasoned, seared and sautéed forever.

To feel the burn,

the burn they scorched their lovers with,

people who trusted them,

people faithful to them,

people obedient to them,

they betrayed the people who loved them.

"Betrayal hurts,

but the pain of beatings and domination,

is what leaves the physical scars.

The place for those souls,

lies not far..."

At the base of the mountains,

the stones are churning,

the bowels of the earth are shaking.

"Push...Push...Push..."

A voice roars,

and the crack of a whip snaps,

we watch from the crest of the mighty cliffs,

as the enslaved souls clench down upon,

a titanic dowel rod, attached to a massive wheel,

running along its track, crushing all in its path.

In front of the slaves that push,

another row of souls bound by chains pull,

this mighty wheel of torture.

Hulking giants slash and whip,

across their backs, pushing them harder,

these domineering souls,

are the top of the food chain no longer.

Upon the huge round altar,

where the stone rolls along,

souls of those that beat and tortured their loved ones,

are smashed into powder and dust.

Men and women, who thought they were in control,

they beat and manipulated their significant others,

and now it is them,

who are being driven down.

The blood flows over,

the crushed skulls and mangled skin,

as the lines pour in closer,

to be bound and crushed forever.

"I know you can think of many,

who deserve to be here.

The women in your life who belittled you,

trampled you under!

They cheated on you, left you cold,

but I'm telling you...just let the anger for them go!"

I was lost in my thoughts,

those...women...those sluts and whores,

they fancied lust over who I was,

I wish...I want to see their faces crushed,

maimed by this giant wheel,

maybe boiled, or skinned and filleted!

"Let it go!" He grabs me by the shoulders.

"Please, I'm telling you, I can sense,

your hatred getting stronger!

These places are meant to help you,

to heal you...make you mend!

The pain you create for yourself in life,

it will lead you into a miserable, isolated end!"

Daniel was right, I feel it,

that anger burning, swelling in me,

this place has given me ideas,

for those I feel deserve,

to feel the pain,

the impact they left on me.

He lets go, and I begin to calm down,

I feel those hurtful thoughts subside,

but they haven't gone away,

even after this grim display.

"I think we need to keep going deeper,

soon...very soon, we will see...

well, let's just continue onwards."

The Chamber of Eyes

-

"We're getting closer to the lower layer,

now, we approach the final chamber.

This is where the eyes saw too much,

and so, they are removed,

be careful, stay quiet or else,

the guardians will take ours too!"

We keep to the high grounds,

as we have done so throughout this journey,

for good reasons, because these voracious bastards,

down here, they have no discrepancies,

between the tortured and the living.

Within these halls, deep in this chamber,

the walls are black and faded over,

with mist and fog, haze and silence,

except for the piercing screams of their blindness.

Guardians surround, crying men and women,

and with their bare hands,

rip out their eyes by the root,

and place them into the walls.

The walls, deep into the black abyss,

the shadows are swallowed,

and bulging out, are the eyes of the watchers,

to forever watch the agony,

of seeing the next corral of souls,

receive their punishment.

They cannot blink, they cannot flinch,

they must watch from the endless abyss.

They cry blood, the tears of crimson red,

to forever see death, to forever witness dread.

"These are the peeping-toms,

the curious, the false readers,

people who could not keep their eyes to themselves,

people who wanted to watch, take pleasure in others pain,

or just take pleasure in spying on others."

"But Daniel...if I may ask,

how is this the worst of this layer?

Worse than sexual deviants, thieves,

or murderers?"

"As we reach the lower layers,

we get closer to the source at the heart,

closer to what made,

the previous atrocities come to pass.

These deviants, these tormented souls,

it all started with a look,

then an idea,

they sized up their mark, and made the decision,

that is how their road to damnation began..."

I pondered this, I understood,

but not sure if I agreed,

I guess, however...judgment is how it begins,

that's how we decide, we choose to attack,

we see a weakness and then we strike,

where its most vulnerable,

this is how we pick our victims,

eyes to thought, thought to planning,

planning to action, and with every action,

there is a consequence, a reaction.

"My inferno was my judgment,

how I depicted with my own vision,

and my own thoughts, this lead to my action,

my creation, my orchestration..." He replies.

Judgment...is a god's will,

we are our own god, we must find,

our own salvation, or else we create,

our own hell...our own damnation.

"Before we head into the deeper layers,

I want you to follow me,

through here, into the mirror's lair..."

The Horror of Mirrors

†

We enter a room, adjacent from the eyes,

where souls are blind, here is where they see,

only what the mirror shows them,

their true self, on the inside,

is what will appear in the glass.

"This room is empty,

only certain souls will pass through here,

they avoided their punishment thus far,

but it is here, where their torment will begin,

as they will see what is within."

First, Daniel stands in front of the mirror,

to show me, what hides from my eyes on the surface,

but underneath, Daniel's true form appears,

he is a beggar, a coward,

lying upon the ground, writhing and terrified,

a weak beggar on the outside and inside.

"I was afraid, I was tempted,

by beasts and demons, I am judged,

on my weakness, afraid to proceed through darkness,

until my guide appeared before me,

and helped me find my way,

the road to forgiveness,

to redeem myself and my faith."

Daniel was a man who lost his way,

but has found some form of peace,

a road to redemption by the choices he made,

to find the light to reach his love,

and feel whole again.

"And now...it is your turn,

stand here and see for yourself,

who...or what, you chose to be..."

Daniel demands to me.

I step forward and close my eyes,

facing the reflection of the glass,

around me I feel...heat,

and into the mirror, into my soul I look,

around me the flames arise,

there among the inferno stands a hulking beast,

ravaged with anger and rage,

loss of control, a monster without peace.

My actions have brought down empires,

left the lives of others in despair and ruin,

a killer, a destroyer, a ravager,

thoughts of slaughter and chaos,

a deep innate drive for revenge and payback.

Jealousy has transformed my emotions,

angst has given me strength and power,

power to destroy, the power to annihilate,

and yet, my reflection,

that beast begins to break down and revert back,

the true horror resonates, a deeper impact within,

my reflection looks at me and cries,

begging for forgiveness at what I have done.

I look down to my own hands,

and the blood, it swells and bleeds over,

the rage of eons, the rage I know now,

it cannot go on any longer.

"Is...is this what I am,

a monster, a blood-thirsty beast?

Is that the true shape that's inside of me?"

Daniel reaches into his robes,

and removes the divine order,

"Here read this...I think it's time, you understand."

> **To Dante,**
> **"This mortal is lost, as you once were,**
> **I have watched him for some time,**
> **and he is on the road to self-destruction.**
>
> **Take him on the path,**
> **as Virgil once showed you,**
> **show him what true hell is like,**
> **I know there is something left inside,**
> **I have sensed it, I have seen it,**
> **help him find what was lost,**
> **help him find what lays deep inside,**
> **an understanding, confidence and peace,**
> **so that he reevaluates his life,**
> **and this place will not be his fate...."**
>
> **- The Father**

"So...do you understand now?

This is not about mere faith and damnation,

those are ideas, points of view,

this hell we walk through,

this is you, this is what you subconsciously go through,

day after day,

this is your realm, your making,

just as we create our own ideas of a heaven,

we also create an alternate place, a hell within us.

There is only the faith, you keep in yourself,

we are our own god and devil,

our own hell and heaven,

just as we have our good days and bad,

we have to somewhere in us,

have a sense of balance and understanding,

to indulge to much in one can lead to the scales tipping,

and we will fall to our own undoing."

"This monster, this cannot be,

this mirror has to be a lie, a trick upon me,

I have had my days and my brutal day-dreams,

but I am not a killer, a rapist, a thief-

I am no creature of this much devastation!"

Daniel lowers his head.

"Denial is the reason for their agony,

as it is for you.

We still have further to go,

we are not through..."

-The Lower Level-

Southern Corridor:
Punish the Dishonored and Cowards

Tongues Ripped Out
-

Beyond these doors,

resides the liars and trouble-makers,

the cowards and the spineless,

the hopeless and the lost.

Within the gates of the Dishonored,

and the Cowards, we will see,

what tortures bring them to agony,

a far worse fate than their existence,

the torture for their self-loathing.

We walk beyond the gates,

of liquid metal doors and waterfalls,

of tears and sweat,

we hear the liars screaming,

these are the souls who tattled and deceived,

only now, to have their voices removed.

"The horrific, twisted mares pull them along,

upon plows to sow these barren fields,

with all the dirt and filth they spoke,

their fibs hydrate,

the root of corruption to others,

grows deep, and upon the plows they pull,

the souls along by their tongues,

and when ripped out,

blood and tears water the soil,

rotten as were their words they spoke."

Wailing bodies are ripped away,

only for another to take their place.

"What happens with the ones taken away?"

I ask.

"Their bodies are thrown into pits,

to be buried over, for this is their fate,

to be buried in their filth,

they dug their ditch with their lies,

and once the soul rots,

it will be devoured by,

the millions of maggots and flies."

Daniel replies.

I turn my eyes away,

the writhing twisted shapes in mud and dirt,

their fate is unbearable to watch,

as they struggle to escape.

Disemboweled
-

"As for the cowards,

their fate gets worse,

for they showed no promise,

no bravery towards those they abandoned,

those they left to suffer, left to fend,

for themselves while they ran away,

deserters who now must pay..."

The crying and the whining,

is unbearable to listen to,

as the guardians scoop them up,

and throw them onto conveyor belts,

and heavy machinery pulls them closer,

towards automated, titanic forks and spoons.

To have their guts ripped out,

their entrails removed.

They hid in the shadows,

now they are moved to,

an area with many surgical lights,

207

as bright as a thousand suns,

where under a mighty surgical dome,

they are dropped,

and the giant forks, spoons and knives,

rip them away and splay them,

taking away the legs, so they cannot run,

remove the arms, so they cannot retaliate,

remove the guts, because they were never brave,

remove the spines, for being spineless in life.

The dome fills up with blood,

after the massacre is done,

and the filters run them through,

out the bottom, and then,

the next batch is run through and dropped in,

to begin again, and again, and again.

"They are trapped within the prison,

the punishment they always escaped,

now here, they can never leave,

they can never get away."

Daniel takes me along,

and we make our way,

to a place where freezers and cold,

seal the fate of misdemeanors,

the trouble-makers,

towards loved ones and friends,

they spurned and hurt,

ones who loved them in return,

and all they showed them,

was a meaningless hate.

Chamber of Ice

-

We walk along,

in a valley of ice and snow,

where in these walls,

the souls are frozen,

children who resented their parents,

family who caused harm to loved ones,

people who harmed elders as caregivers,

are frozen away into a catatonic state,

where their minds eternally play,

what they did wrong.

I look into one of these prisms,

their naked bodies are trapped,

in a state of pain and exposed,

to the cruel life they made,

as the bitter cold, the bitter words,

slowly, eternally, peels them away.

"Their words chipped and cracked,

the foundations of their relationships,

and now they are the ones,

that will fall to pieces."

Massive cyclopean beings,

with titanic hammers rumble along,

to those who are frozen like statues,

out in the open, are shattered,

as the mighty cudgels slam down,

and break them into pieces.

The glass and ice shards scatter,

as do we, we move on,

into the next plane,

where eternal sadness reigns.

Together,

Daniel and I,

we cross a lone bridge,

of ancient wood over,

a pit of sludge and oil,

"The Town of Suicide,

next exit...one mile"

Reads the sign upon the outer edge,

of the rim where the sadness,

and the self-loathing go,

to wallow and walk along in confusion,

not sure of which way is home.

The town is old and worn,

lost in a sea of fog and floods,

the ones who took their own life,

don't remember what life was,

who they were, or why they're here,

all they know is the pain of despair.

"Look at them,

they are those who altered the lines of fate,

they lost all hope, for them,

these lost souls, it was too late.

Images of their family and loved ones,

try to console them, but the faces,

are blurred and obscure,

they know no love, no belonging,

as in life, they were lost,

and forever they wander this town,

to aimlessly walk among a haze of confusion,

and puddles of tears."

"I know the feeling all too well," I reply.

"I know the thoughts of wanting to escape,

the cowardice of just giving up,

and wanting to die..."

And it starts to rain upon us,

as the living mourn their lost here,

wanting to know the reasons,

of why they left so soon.

"They left their loved ones,

in confusion as well as eternal sorrow,

for this plane of hell stretches beyond,

the doors of infinity,

and into the hearts and minds of others,

that still remember their lives,

while these souls do not..."

Some hang up by the knot,

some wallow in pools of water,

some pick the scabs from their wrists,

some...some are so young,

they never experienced their first kiss.

"The feeling of helplessness,

affects us all in times of grief and despair,

but you cannot let it over come you,

or else, you wind up here.

Among the ruins of time,

and the shattered boundaries of life,

here all has stopped, all is silent,

only the sounds of the suffering,

of the ones that still mourn..."

To see these blank faces,

and the tears in the eyes of mothers,

fathers, brothers, sisters, friends,

and family, their grief,

it's not worth the price,

of a cheap escape.

We leave these ruins,

and let the weeping stay behind,

as we begin the final descent,

still we go downwards,

beyond the boundaries of this city,

resides the forests and the caves of madness,

where confusion and mental instability,

is kept separated,

locked away from all the others.

"What lies in there,

where the shadows are darkest?"

I ask.

He lowers his head,

"There is only one soul within this place,

let us go and meet him,

just let him do the talking, and listen,

but you will not like his ways,

they may hit closer to home with you.

You'll see things in the flesh,

you may dismay, you will feel enraged,

agitated and ashamed..."

He looks at me,

"For this is a place,

specific for you,

this is the home,

these trees and caves, mountains and valleys,

they are your thoughts and feelings,

lost and confused, confined to this maze."

The Shadow's King

†

We traverse on down these sullen steps,

of valleys and tunnels, to deeper depths,

to the kingdom where the shadows lay,

and the keeper of this darkness stays.

"Within these halls,

buried under this fortress,

of black skies and opaque waves,

this is where the court of the Shadow King,

writhes within his mental anguish and disdain."

We walk across marble brick,

black as stained earth and the stench,

of a foul, stale breeze,

is frozen here, with all time for eternity.

Upon his throne, the king in black sits,

his head bowed, covered over,

by the shadow of his crown,

a diadem of ebony and coal,

smoke arises from the floor,

not of heat but of sorrow,

a putrid smoke he inhales forever,

and we take a hit, a sting upon the tongue,

a burn upon our voices,

a suffocation of our lungs,

sweet and deadly, plentiful and steady,

wave after wave of shadows we consume,

as we step closer and closer,

to the lord of gloom.

Daniel and I, we stand before his throne,

and he awakens, he looks up at us,

and as I look into those eyes,

into that...that face...

what do I see? For the Shadow king,

he looks a lot like me!

And yet...he does not roar,

he does not shout or scream,

he holds out his hand, towards two black chairs,

of twisted steel and black bars,

he speaks softly,

"Ah...visitors. Please, have a seat."

We bow in return, confusion upon my face,

yet, Daniel does not say anything,

he bows, and I bow with him,

he says, *"Thank you, King."*

And we have a seat, and listen,

to what he has to say.

"It has, been some time, maybe never,

since I laid eyes upon faces,

had any visitors. I...I can't quite remember..."

"We've come to..." I say, he cuts me off with a snap,

"DID I GIVE YOU PERMISSION TO SPEAK?!"

He screams,

"I...please forgive me,

but let's be honest for once,

it is my voice who speaks then answers,

I only want to hear what I have to say...

A game of chess? Does anyone want to play?"

I look at Daniel, terrified and afraid,

he replies in a whisper,

"This is a soul who has spent his entire existence,

within solitary confinement,

no friends and his own worst enemy,

he has only ever spoken to himself,

of himself, about himself,

and he does not like what he hears,

about what his other side says...

but, I suggest you play...go ahead."

I nod, and agree to a game with the King,

he descends the throne,

and shuffles across the floor,

he grasps the table,

and places it in front of where we are.

A lavish, marble table,

of ebony and ivory,

the conflicting sides of good or bad,

right or wrong, dark and light,

night and day...heaven and hell,

the damned...and the saved.

"Shall we play? I white...and you,

my challenger, you'll be black?"

I say ok, and the game is underway.

"As white...I shall go first," and,

he moves his first pawn forward.

I place my pawn in front of his,

knight moves up, then over,

it's now my decision...isn't it...

No rooks nor knights,

bishops remain in waiting,

the queen stands next to her king,

as the impatience upon *His* face grows,

He's waiting.

I move another pawn one space,

as he repeats, the black nails grip,

upon the ivory soldier,

and that soldier's fate, his end,

grows closer.

Knight then bishop, I'm in the line of fire,

bring back my soldier,

keep him out of harm's way,

as I take on the role of defender.

Pawn against pawn,

as the game goes on, the first is mine,

and so the war has begun.

"So...what brings a mortal man,

of living flesh and blood,

and a spirit of ancient days,

all the way down, into this place,

of emptiness and darkened days?"

I give no reply,

only a look of concentration,

keeping my eyes on my soldiers,

protecting my kingdom.

"Go on...answer.

You may speak now,

I give you permission."

I keep my patience steady,

with this, such a selfish.

loathing being.

I answer politely.

"Why are we here, you ask me.

How to answer? Well,

I suppose you could say,

I've been chosen..."

And he shifts the pieces, the tables turned,

as he collects my rook and slays my bishop.

"I should let you know...

this is my game...my rules,

light conquers darkness in the scheme of things,

the thread of destiny is tied to whether or not,

I succeed...and you...you will, I'm afraid,

will fail."

Cheating bastard, a sore loser,

within his many moves, I retaliate,

and then, something strange takes place,

the battlefield shifts and warps,

as we no longer reside within these caves,

transported across time and space,

and placed upon a battlefield of death and decay.

Where pawns and rooks, knights and bishops,

in armor head to foot, slaughter and kill,

as the blood and bodies pile up,

and the grass has its fill of blood and gore.

There I stand upon the hill,

and by my side, a queen dressed in black,

with royal armor, her sword is drawn,

as I the King, she protects,

as the armies in white charge on,

to check me and take my head.

The screams of the dead and deafening battle,

passes under many days and many moons,

as day turns to night, noon shifts to twilight.

My queen, she smiles,

"Don't worry, my King...by life or death,

I will protect you."

Waves of ivory wash over,

with waves of red, splattered over,

with gore and guts across their armor,

but my soldiers dwindle,

the pawns have been all but spent,

and the leftovers linger in agony,

deformed and mutilated beyond comprehension.

"Why am I here?"

I ask myself, I'm here to beat this darkness,

and see things in a different light,

forgiveness of myself and my actions,

fighting a war that goes on and on,

fighting a constant battle that needs to be won.

I draw my sword,

in this game, when desperation sinks in,

the best way to strengthen the odds,

either way, it's loose or win,

the King must enter the battle,

put aside fear, and join in.

225

"What are you doing?!"

My queen cries aloud with horror.

I gather the last of my nights and rooks together,

"We charge! Onward!"

Pawns strike to their left and to their right,

rooks rush across the grass in a straight line,

knights break away, up and then left and right,

bishops head in diagonal directions,

while the queen stays by my side,

as we spill the blood with crimson tides,

we carve our way to the king and his white crown,

to bring down the false hope, the lies, the scapegoat,

we muster on the offensive,

to bring the Shadow King down.

Pawns jump knights,

bishops hack white rooks into pieces,

the queen stands her ground,

slaughtering all who attack from the rear,

and through the hordes, the Shadow King appears.

226

I never saw it coming,

and neither did she,

the shadows hurdle over,

and with the King's hammer,

my queen is crushed, as she topples,

her flesh and bone crumbles to the ground.

The Shadow King raises the hammer again,

to plunge and strike me down,

I turn, and with the slash of my blade,

I check the King and bring him to the ground.

The world shifts and alters,

twists and turns about,

shades writhe with agony, as they are swept away,

and we return, sitting within this silent room,

and before my eyes sits,

the chess board covered in blood and bone,

pieces of soldiers and warriors now gone.

The Shadow King sighs,

"Well...looks like you checked my king,

congratulations, you won...

a great game of chess you play, I must say..."

And he gets up and walks away,

my darkened self, he lost the battle,

but the war is not over it seems,

as Daniel places his hand upon my shoulders,

it's time to move on into the next plane.

"Congratulations,

you showed courage and perseverance,

bravery, although a bit brutal,

but you showed him, you showed the Shadow King.

We all must loose sometimes,

but from our loses, along the way,

we will also have our victories.

Now come, we still have more to see,

your closer, young poet,

your closer to seeing the light in the day."

"What about him?"

I ask.

"Let him be, let him linger,

he will feel the disappointment,

but the important thing is what you won here,

how do you feel?"

How do I feel?
"I feel stronger, more confident,

a hint of bravery, that as impossible,

the battle was, I came out more dedicated,

and the winner."

"You never were a braggart,

and that is good, I say you did win,

stay humble and never lose sight,

that through the darkness there is still light."

He leads me along.
"Come, we must be on our way,

the final chambers are ahead of us,

the shadow of yourself will remain here to stay,

just...don't let him stay with you."

Deepest Corridor:
Torture the Cruel and the Tyrants

The Chamber of Burden

"Is there a devil?"

I ask Daniel.

He looks at me,

"As I have said before, the devil, like god,

is something we keep inside ourselves.

Our thoughts of hate and jealousy,

revenge and wrong-doing,

our greed and lust,

these are all just a part of a larger enigma,

the paradox of thoughts and feelings,

every man and woman, keeps within their heart.

Each vessel a chamber, a place we keep,

the pieces of ourselves,

our feelings and emotions.

So, in answer to your question,

is there a devil in the flesh? The answer,

is no...there is only the devil,

we create as a reflection in our image,

our darker selves."

The mirrors and the shadows,

the chambers and the punishment,

it all makes sense, it all makes,

just a little more sense.

I ponder in thought, for this has always made sense,

we reflect upon others,

what we see in ourselves, that we can't stand.

And those piercing screams and cries,

have subsided, for down here,

no one can hear the screams, so why bother,

these are the catacombs of guilt and regret,

where the crimes against humanity,

the criminals of disgusting, destructive acts,

can never redeem and forever regret,

for they are trapped here,

in these places they are kept.

"Here, their screams within,

echo louder than any others,

lifetimes long and brief,

of their atrocities towards human beings,

see there, upon the mighty stone pillars..."

He points, and there they stand,

the souls of mothers and fathers,

who abandoned their children,

the life they brought into the world,

responsibilities they could not bear,

and here they forever carry the burden,

as it drives them downwards.

Some they raised to be criminals,

some were raised as murderers,

some they abandoned as infants,

neglected the precious gift of life,

they let fade away.

"Here is where it all begins,

with the mother and the father,

some smother and some neglect,

232

the burden of rocks and boulders,

are given to them, by the size of their crimes,

to carry upon their shoulders,

as a reminder...a guilt for all time.

Some of these children they raised,

into addicts, some lost control,

and morphed through life into abusers and molesters,

they harmed themselves and or brought pain to others."

I recognize the woman, the tormented soul,

whom we met at the beginning,

standing before the judges at the gates,

here is where her fate remains.

She bears upon her thin arms,

the massive boulder pressed down upon her,

by the weight and the guilt,

of the child she left to drown, left to die,

irresponsible and not ready for the burden,

of raising a human life.

Fathers who beat their children,

feel the pressure more,

the pain they inflicted upon their children,

their bodies are pushed down more and more.

Soon, they will lose their grip,

lose control, as they lost control of themselves,

and they stumble and fall,

into the pits of foul sludge and oceans of decay below.

"Some of these children became dictators and tyrants,

they caused war and famine, death and genocide,

creating machinations of extermination,

their canvas was the world,

and they painted it with the blood of many,

built their palaces with flesh and bone,

labor and suffering,

from slaves as they watched upon their thrones.

But for them...there is another place they go."

It all started with the parents,

these parents stand upon the pillars of stone,

as the burden of life, wears them down,

and makes them weak and old.

Their weak will cannot hold these rocks forever,

and soon they will fall into these oceans and rivers,

to drown in their sorrow, of the seas they fill.

It all starts with guidance, a duty,

they never fulfilled.

All they had to do, was show their child love,

help them understand and judge right and wrong,

but they abandoned their burdens upon others,

and it's others that suffered for where they went wrong.

The Final Chamber
-

And so,

we come at last,

to the final chamber.

Boarded up by steel and welded shut,

guarded by soldiers with machineguns,

and sentries scorching flamethrowers.

They cut us off,

"Halt...you will proceed no further!

For beyond this door,

within these halls,

the tyrants and genocidal maniacs,

suffer as their existence and souls dissolve!"

A stalwart and vicious guardian calls.

Daniel steps forward,

"You will let us pass,

it is our right, we are granted by Divine Order!"

They pay no heed,

and the guards step forward,

guns raised, their target in sight,

and...I gasp in horror!

As waves of bullets fire,

and Daniel Gerry, the poet of yesteryear,

his robes tear and shred,

as the creator of the Divine Comedy,

my guide, his time within this place,

has expired.

I fall to my knees,

and kneel by his side,

as a bright light erupts from within,

and his spirit is carried upwards.

"It's...it's up to you now...

shall you stand your ground,

and proceed further,

or shall the fear take hold,

and all you've seen,

all you've learned,

shall dissolve, and my guidance,

my sacrifice, will be for nothing..."

These are his last words,

before he is taken back,

to be with his lost love,

beyond the gates of the divine.

"Stand down mortal,

your flesh is of the living,

heed our warning,

if you try to proceed,

we'll make sure you'll never leave,

and your soul will rot here for eternity!"

"Turn back, and go the way you came,

face your mortality, and accept your fate!"

"You're time will come mortal,

and we'll be waiting,

we'll be waiting..."

He lowers the gun,

and returns to his post,

their glaring eyes upon me,

watching...waiting...

observing what I'm doing.

And so I wander along,

I sit and ponder,

there must be a way in,

there must be a way out,

for I belong here no longer.

That's when a thought occurs to me,

maybe there's a slight chance,

that my darker self, my doppelganger,

maybe I can get the one in the shadows,

to help me?

Return to the Shadows
†

And so I travel back,

alone and burdened,

not knowing what will happen next,

not knowing what to expect.

Of all those tales of traveling through hell,

which of them has ever gone back?

I pass through the chamber of burden,

and this time, without my guide,

the mountains and the ruins,

feel harder to climb.

Back through the valleys of night,

back into the darkness where there is no light,

and the shadows of the king begin to arise,

as he stands upon the rocky summit,

above all the forests and planes of darkness,

as though he were expecting me,

his other self walks into sight.

I climb the summit,

stone by stone I arise,

to meet my altered shadow,

the king of darkness I caused demise.

I face me, for the second time,

on terms of which, I don't know what,

I just know if I'm to escape,

me and we...we must join together,

and find that middle ground,

a form of compromise,

for both shadow and grey,

only then can we once more,

see the white.

"I don't know why,

but I knew you'd return,

be it fate or by coincidence,

there is a larger role for us both at hand."

I reply,

"The way is shut,

there is no getting through,

but maybe...just maybe,

if we work together,

there may be a chance."

"What did you have in mind?"

We sit and speak for a while,

we have time, and I have a plan,

that we and I, can both agree on.

The Final Chamber Opens
†

The Shadow King approaches the gates,

he pulls back his hood to reveal my face,

the guardians confused take a second look,

they know it's me, at least,

an element of what I am to be.

"We warned you once,

and we won't do so again,

back away, or else,

you shall share the same fate,

as the one we already put down!"

And the Shadow King speaks,

"Gentleman, guardians of the gates,

shall you but for a moment,

put your weapons down,

and join me in a little game?

If you lose, I go through,

but if you win,

I guess it's my soul then."

And he brings forward,

the cleaned and polished chess board,

as the guardians mock this jest,

with a look of scorn.

"Mortal! We have no time for games,

for its these souls of death and destruction,

these beings that have caused the most vile acts,

of genocide and deicide,

they are the ones that have caused the most pain!

It is these...wretched beings,

we must keep at bay!

As for you and your games,

I give you one last warning,

walk away...or your mortal coil,

we shall have the pleasure of splaying,

and sticking you up on display!"

And the guns are aimed,

ready to blast the Shadow King away.

And I watch from the shadows,

as the Shadow King wields his powers,

and the visions of battle and slaughter,

begin to shift and alter,

as the guardians are drawn in,

to face the resurrected legions of the Shadow King,

he laughs as he turns to me,

"They'll be busy for a while, as the games begin!"

That's my cue, and I dart across the battle field,

through the rapid fire of guns and bullets,

as the guardians mow the pawns and rooks down,

but behind the waves of the crooked crosses,

the malevolent bishops and the white queen,

covered in blood and cracks from war,

swarm the guardians and surround their perimeter.

I reach the doors, but there is no lock,

there is neither key nor winch to open them up,

that is until, a huge explosion,

a blast from the guardian fires at me,

it misses as I leap away, and within the doors,

a huge, gaping hole is created,

I slip away from the battle,

and through the crack into the final chamber,

I leap in.

"BOOOOOOM!"

Behind me, a huge mushroom cloud rises up,

as the battle field is nuked,

and the silence of extermination falls,

no more shall the King's Horses,

no more shall the King's minions,

rise up again.

There among the dissipating clouds,

and the smoke that clears,

among the bodies of the guardians and the soldiers,

there stands only one,

through the fog and ashes,

the Shadow King appears.

He says,

"Continue onwards,

I stay here to pick up the pieces,

of all this destruction and domination,

that we have caused,

for someone has to take responsibility,

for what we have done."

"For what we've done…"

We're both here for what we've done,

the ruin we caused for ourselves and others,

our thoughts and actions,

the distress we've caused to ourselves,

has always been spreading outwards.

Within this final chamber,

further on downwards,

is where I'll find,

the tyrants and their warring ways,

the excuse of greater good,

may have fooled the surface,

but not down here,

within this final chamber,

is where the tyrants face their ultimate fear.

There is no tree, nor blade of grass,

there is only liquid fire and napalm,

from their nuclear holocaust.

There is no wind, nor rain or sun,

there is only corrosion and poison gas,

exhumed from the corpses of their victims,

after the atomic aftermath blew them up.

There are no buildings,

within this dungeon,

where the tyrants are chased by mobs,

as they struggle to run,

while upon their backs,

they carry loaded shells of their missiles and bombs.

The roaring mobs of angered souls,

torn to pieces by the greed and wrath,

of these tyrants' warpath,

they chase them down one by one,

and beat their prey down into the fallout mush,

before the fear of the tyrants take hold,

and that's when the bomb goes off,

and within the blast, all flesh explodes.

"These are the ultimate cowards,

the conquering thieves, the desecraters of life,

destroyers of the weak, and the murderers of many,

of all the wars they caused,

leading millions to their demise."

The only difference with them,

is they feel nothing,

no regret inside, and once the soul is blown away,

it becomes one with the pollution,

the acid in this putrid soil,

the shit of the world that spoils,

and with the rest of the garbage,

is burned away.

These are the ones,

the alphas of the world,

they are the ones who got too greedy,

and started it all!

For many of these souls,

are here because of them,

a war between a ruling body,

and her people,

a war of rich against poor,

fortunate against the weak,

a war that shall rage for eternity."

This realm, these chambers,

the hell of ourselves, that we keep,

a voracious cycle within us,

can we ever stop it,

will the vices that bring us pain,

ever cease?

I pass across the world of war,

a place that isn't so far away,

closer to home, closer than you may think,

trudging across the bile of famine,

the oceans of blood and lives,

the seas of generals,

the commanders and the conquerors,

who gave nothing but took everything,

all the residue from countless eons of brutality,

but, after all, this is our culture,

this is humankind and our bestiality.

I pass far beyond the rim,

of the plateaus and the barren shores,

across the way and far over there,

over the hills and mountains of death and decay,

there sits in the cracks of these walls,

a lone and somber door.

For so long, I've spent in hell,

is it just so easy,

to walk out the door?

The things I've seen,

all the screaming,

all the suffering,

all the death and decay,

will I be sane enough,

to face the world today?

Am I strong enough,

to walk out that door today?

I feel that I am,

I've learned a few lessons to proceed,

to try to be a better me, I mean after all,

I've seen where the world is going,

what terrors they make for themselves,

because in reality,

all the disturbing images we've seen,

is it any different from the behavior we witness,

of those up there still living,

on the news, over the web,

and our own personal meanings,

of the ones that call themselves, normal,

responsible human beings?

-Out from Darkness-

Outside the Chamber:
Recollection of an Existence

Keep the Dour Closed
-

What have I learned?

While me and my guide,

have wandered across wastelands,

worlds of decay and torment,

within the minds of my own inner workings?

I've seen the darkest of shadows,

the burn of malicious hate,

the cold of the forgotten and the abandoned,

within this hellish no-man's land.

And the door continues to rattle,

and the door continues to shake,

until the chains snap,

and the locks melt away.

And so I open the door,

and walk outside into a familiar land,

but deep within I'm a little different,

the same world but a different man,

I've learned a valuable lesson,

but alas, it's a lesson that only I can understand.

What have I learned...

while traveling through hell and coming back?

A lesson that when we try a little bit harder,

and try to be a little bit better,

release the hate and let go the anger,

I've learned, that sometimes in life,

you have to go through hell,

to get stronger.

I think it's better to open up,

and proceed further,

than keep the door closed,

and hold in all the fears and struggles,

we don't want to be exposed.

On the Other Side
-

I walk outside,

but there is no light,

no rays of sunshine,

only a heavy rain,

that seeps from the gray skies.

The ground is moist,

the land slants and leans,

this is no exit,

no escape it seems.

I feel weary,

and so I lay down and go to sleep,

I drift back into delirium,

into ancient memories,

clouded over by twilight.

Ahead of me,

I see,

a yawning void,

a whirlwind of rage and insanity.

I begin to hear those familiar sounds,

it's all coming back to me,

I begin to remember,

there was never a heaven or hell...

Only paranoia and anxiety,

brought on by the vices of reality.

A deadly sphere...of repetition and continuity.

Out from hell, I arise from the abyss,

cast upon a land of elements,

a land of sorrows, a plane of rapture and weakness,

a vast and turning sphere of influence...

www.ingramcontent.com/pod-product-compliance
Lightning Source LLC
LaVergne TN
LVHW041315080426
835513LV00008B/464